*f*P

THREE QUARTERS, TWO DIMES, AND A NICKEL

❈

A MEMOIR OF BECOMING WHOLE

Steve Fiffer

THE FREE PRESS

*f*P

THE FREE PRESS
A Division of Simon & Schuster Inc.
1230 Avenue of the Americas
New York, NY 10020

Portions of this book appeared previously in
The New York Times Magazine and Chicago Tribune Magazine

Designed by Jennifer Dossin

Manufactured in the United States of America

1 3 5 7 9 10 8 6 5 4 2

Library of Congress Cataloging-in-Publication Data
Fiffer, Steve.
Three quarters, two dimes, and a nickel: a memoir of becoming
whole / Steve Fiffer.
      p.   cm.
1. Fiffer, Steve—Health. 2. Neck—Wounds and injuries—Patients—United
States—Biography. I. Title.
RD796.F54A3   1998   98-47403   CIP
362.4'3'092—dc21
[B]
ISBN 0-684-85418-X

FOR MY PARENTS

AUTHOR'S NOTE

This is a true story. That said, I wish to inform the reader of the following: Many of the events described in this book took place over thirty years ago. I have tried my best to accurately re-create all scenes and conversations and to portray all individuals as I remember them. In some instances, I have changed the names of characters or the details of their lives and, in a few instances, I have created composite characters. Finally, for the purpose of telling the story logically, coherently, and dramatically, I have in some instances combined two or more events from different time frames into a single event. None of these changes are material to or alter the ultimate truth of the story.

He who hurries cannot walk with dignity.

CHINESE PROVERB

PROLOGUE

In the 1950s and 1960s when I was growing up, there were two mortal sins of which a Chicagoan could be guilty: being a Republican and rooting for the New York Yankees. If I had been old enough, I would have voted the straight Democratic ticket as my parents did at each election. No trouble there. But, Father, forgive me, I was a Yankee fan.

As the hometown White Sox were always finishing second to the hated Bronx Bombers, my friends showered me with charges of desertion. I barely heard them. I had the radio to my ear so I could hear Casey Stengel's boys win another World Series. Looking back now, I realize that Freud and Spock be damned, it was the Yankees that shaped my growth. I never learned to accept losing because the Yankees of my childhood so rarely lost.

My life revolved around the team. My favorite color was "pinstripe." My favorite number was 7—after my hero Mickey Mantle, of course. My favorite city, after New York, was Commerce, Oklahoma, the Mick's hometown.

I did all the things a fan eight hundred miles from his idols could do. I saw the Yankees every time they came to town. I sent away for their yearbook. I scoured the public library for books about the team, living in constant fear that some diehard Sox fan would attempt to have such material banned. Two things consumed me: Mantle and the Tradition. I knew everything there was to know about Mickey, and was surely Chicago's leading authority on the Yankees' history that seemed embodied in the House That Ruth Built, Yankee Stadium.

But as rewarding as it was to have my heroes in the World Series each fall, I was frustrated. More than anything else, I wanted Mickey Mantle's autograph. And more than anything except getting the autograph, I wanted to see a game in Yankee Stadium. In the spring of 1959, a few months short of my ninth birthday, I set out to reach those goals.

Getting Mantle's signature was my first priority. I thought long and hard about how to achieve this. I had already tried waiting outside Comiskey Park when the Yanks were in Chicago. No luck. My friend Renslow Sherer—everyone called him Rensy—suggested that Mickey probably snuck out in a disguise, as heavyweight champion Floyd Patterson was wont to do, but I knew I would have recognized him no matter what the costume. I reasoned that there must be a secret passage out of the ballpark reserved for the Williamses and Mantles so they wouldn't get crushed.

Rensy understood the problems in rooting for an out-of-town team. He was the only Milwaukee Braves fan in our class. (Maybe the two of us went against the flow because we were lefties.) He suggested I wait at the hotel where the Yankees stayed. But my father, tolerant as he was of my fixation, refused to spend a day in some lobby on the off chance that the Commerce Comet would be sighted.

I finally decided to write him. I was composing the letter

when the brainstorm struck. Why not invite Mickey for dinner? It must be hard on players when they travel. They miss all that great home cooking that gives them the strength to go out and hit home runs. It must be lonely, too, away from the family. "We are a terrific family, and my mom is a terrific cook," I wrote Mickey. "You can come anytime and she will prepare whatever you want. She makes an excellent Yankee pot roast."

I sent the letter off (as well as letters to every other Yankee—autograph request only, no dinner invitation), convinced that our household would soon be hosting the most famous visitor our neighborhood had ever seen, that soon I'd be seated across the table from my hero, passing the ketchup while hearing what it was like to be a Yankee. If Rensy was nice, I might invite him—for dessert.

While waiting for Mickey to respond with his choice of evening and menu, I attempted to orchestrate my second wish—seeing a game at Yankee Stadium. In late April, I suggested that we should take our annual end-of-the-summer vacation out East, say in the Bronx. The "out East" part of the proposal was quickly adopted, with the caveat that the date of the visit to New York would be contingent on when my father could get away from his law office; the Yankees might be out of town.

I didn't protest. There was no baseball team in the Wisconsin Dells, the second vacation choice. Besides, if there was any justice in the world, a fan as loyal as I would be rewarded.

In May, the Yankees made their first of three trips to Chicago. Mickey had not responded to the invitation, a state of affairs I chose to blame on the U.S. Mail or the fact that the Yankees were off to a slow start. Mickey probably wanted to come to the house when things were looking up.

When the Yanks returned several weeks later, they were still several games out of first place. Still, I had begun to hear from some of the players. Bob Turley. Duke Maas. But not Mantle. Did pitchers have more time to write? Was it a mistake to mention that my mother's specialty was pot roast?

Vacation time approached. My dad had business to conduct in Boston and didn't know if we'd be in New York when the Yankees were there. I didn't know if I could stand the double disappointment of being stood up by Mantle and missing Yankee Stadium. Make that a triple disappointment. Listening to the games on the way east (my Yankees' yearbook had a complete list of radio stations carrying the team's games), it became clear that the Bombers were going to lose their first pennant since 1954 and that the hated White Sox might succeed them.

Still, the Yankees dominated my consciousness. On the road, my younger brother Jim and I played a game in which we tried to guess how much everything cost—food, gas, lodging. Our parents found this gauche and ordered us to stop. But we developed a special code using Yankees' uniform numbers. If we thought gas would cost $4.25, we'd say, "Gehrig-Crosetti-DiMaggio." If the food was "Lopez-Ruth-Berra," Dad had shelled out $11.38.

The hotel in New York must have cost at least Casey Stengel dollars a night. We had adjoining rooms on an upper floor overlooking Central Park. If I could have opened a window, I might have jumped. The Yankees were out of town. I brooded so much that first day, if my father could have opened a window, he might have thrown me out.

On our second morning in the city, I returned from a walk with my mother and brother to find Dad holding his camera and looking very proud of himself. "I called Yankee Stadium and told them I had the greatest fan outside of New York," he said. "And they invited us to come down and see the ballpark."

An hour later we were sitting in the same dugout that Ruth, DiMaggio, and now Mantle had sat in. I walked out onto the field, ran to center. I read the plaques in the outfield and posed for a picture with the batboy (wishing like anything I could have his job). I played a make-believe game of baseball with my brother.

When we got back to Chicago, there was a letter. "This will acknowledge receipt of your recent communication," the message on Yankees' letterhead read. "It is a pleasure to receive such encouraging mail. Thank you for your interest in the Yankees which you have demonstrated by taking the time to write. Sincerely yours. . . ."

It was signed "Mickey Mantle."

There was no mention of my dinner invitation, but I didn't care. I had my autograph and the memories of that day in the Bronx.

After all, how many people can say they have played in Yankee Stadium?

The next day, I invited Rensy to play catch and see the letter. He held it lovingly and said that maybe he'd invite Braves' third baseman Eddie Mathews to dinner. Then we grabbed our gloves and went outside to re-create the last two World Series, which had pitted his Braves against my Yanks.

Spahn on the mound facing Mantle. The Mick lofts a long one to center field.

I tossed the ball in the air as high as I could. It seemed to float up into the cloudless blue sky forever. Long enough for me to think that life would never be any better than this.

I was right. And I was wrong.

PART ONE

This 17 year old male was well until 12/6/67 when while wrestling in gym class in high school he was thrown over and fell on his back and the boy he was wrestling with fell on top of his head coming down at the apex of the neck and chest area. The head was forced upward and the boy felt immediate lack of ability to move his arms or legs. He was unable to continue or move after that and (had) some pain in his neck and very little feeling over the rest of his body and could not move. He was placed on a stretcher and brought to the E.R.

Highland Park Hospital medical records

CHAPTER I

This is what I remember:

My gym teacher, Mr. Hurley, blowing his whistle.

My friend and wrestling partner, Rensy, dipping down to the balding rubber mat and grabbing my right leg at the knee.

Hopping backward on my left foot, both my hands holding onto Rensy's shoulders for balance.

Losing that balance and falling backward toward the ground, my hands still in front of me.

Hitting the mat without breaking my fall.

Knowing immediately that I couldn't move.

Yelling "Get off!"

Mr. Hurley blowing his whistle again, then yelling that no one should touch me.

Rensy saying he was sorry.

The school trainer asking me what part of my body he was pinching.

Not knowing.

Mr. Hurley saying that this was just shock and that I'd be fine in a little while.

Rensy saying he was sorry.

Feeling cold.

The trainer telling someone to get a blanket.

Feeling thirsty.

The trainer refusing to let anyone get me a cup of water because "we don't want to lift his head."

Praying that the paramedics wouldn't drop my stretcher.

Wondering why the ambulance didn't have its siren on.

Asking if the trainer would move from the front of the ambulance and sit next to me in the back.

Stopping.

Someone opening the door.

Hearing my mother's smoker's cough. Hearing our pediatrician, Dr. Kaplan, ask me, "What happened, Jim?" Reminding him that Jim was my younger brother, that my name was Steve.

Dr. Kaplan apologizing.

Seeing the doctor put his hand in mine.

Not being able to feel his hand.

Not being able to squeeze his fingers.

Dr. Kaplan saying he was going to hit my knee with his reflex hammer.

Thinking I felt a dull thud.

Knowing there was no reflex.

Wondering how long it took for shock to wear off.

.   .   .

My mother had just finished her second unfiltered Camel when several men and women dressed in hospital whites and blues, greens and grays, rushed past her to the snowy driveway outside the entrance to the Emergency Room at Highland Park Hospital. One of the men was pushing a cart draped with a white linen sheet.

I had asked Mr. Hurley to call my father at his office in down-town Chicago instead of my mother at home in Glencoe. I knew she was busy taking care of my two younger brothers, Jim and Tommy, who were sick with the flu. On the phone, the gym teacher had lied that my condition was not serious, and my fa-ther had relayed this assessment to Mom. Thus, it didn't occur to her that the ER crew was waiting for *me*. And it didn't regis-ter that I was aboard the red and white ambulance that was crawling up the drive in their direction. As the ambulance door swung open, she looked over out of curiosity, not concern. *Who else is being brought here today?* she wondered.

Then she saw the legs. My legs. Huge as ever—thick as fire hydrants, she always said—with light blond hair, downy as a baby chick's.

A young man dressed, oddly she thought, in a tan parka and white pants slowly climbed out of the back of the ambulance. The school trainer. My mother had seen a helpless expression like his only once before—a dozen years earlier when my dad had emerged, pale as an eggshell, from a hospital room to an-nounce that his father had just died.

The legs coming out of the ambulance now weren't moving. The feet were bare.

She took a deep breath. The dry winter air mixed with the smoke still in her lungs to produce a cough which caught the attention of several of those hovering by the ambulance. "I'm his mother," she said to no one in particular as she moved as close to me as possible. "What happened, honey?"

The deep confident voice that had dominated the dinner table, that had won several debate tournaments for New Trier East High School, that had even been scheduled to represent teenagers across America on a radio show asking Vice President Hubert Humphrey about the war in Vietnam, was so weak that she could barely hear the answer. The next thing she knew, Dr. Kaplan was instructing me to catch his reflex hammer. Her heart dropped with it as it hit the ground, untouched.

.   .   .

"Try and catch this," Dr. Kaplan had said, dropping the reflex hammer between my fingers like my Uncle Bud used to drop a dollar bill at family gatherings—"If you can grab it, the money's yours." I think aerodynamics made it impossible to catch the dollar. Something else prevented me from catching the hammer.

"That's okay, honey."

I could see through my mom's smile. "I had a feeling something like this was going to happen," I said. "Things were just going too smoothly."

What was the worst thing that had ever happened to me? Being second-string instead of first-string soccer goalie? Getting a C in advanced geometry? Breaking up with Randi? I'd never even been to a funeral. Something had to give.

They took X-rays of my neck and back. A man in a white jacket appeared at my side, but, unable to move my head, I couldn't see his face. He told a nurse to take my pulse and blood pressure, and then take my temperature, and I could tell from his voice that he was in charge. He told someone to cut off my gym clothes and added something about a Foley catheter.

The jacket moved to my head, leaned over, and the voice finally had a face—a tan, weathered face with steely gray eyes and bushy eyebrows the color of ash. Red script over a pocket read: Dr. R. Meyer. "How ya' doin', pal?" he asked.

I tried to reach for the thermometer in my mouth, but my

arm didn't get the message. Dr. Meyer did. I liked him. "I'm okay," I said.

"So you're a wrestler, huh?"

"No, sir. Soccer player. We were wrestling in gym class."

"Well, that's quite a pair of legs you got. What can you do with them for me?"

"Make them play dead?" I tried to smile. "Is my dad here?"

"Not yet."

I sensed someone was doing something at my midsection, but I couldn't see or feel what was going on. "I'm supposed to be on a radio show with Vice President Humphrey on Monday—"

Dr. Meyer anticipated my question. "We'll have to see. We're going to put you in traction for a while so your head won't move around."

They slid me onto what they called a Circolectric bed. It was more like a tilt board, slanted to keep me almost upright. They put sandbags by my arms and legs so I wouldn't slide off.

My world expanded. I could now see that there were four other people in the room—Dr. Meyer, two nurses, and an orderly. Also in scope, hanging at my side, was a clear plastic bag that was slowly filling with a light yellow liquid. A tube extended from the bag. Dr. Meyer sensed my concern. He explained that the tube was called a catheter and that it was draining my bladder.

"How'd it get to my bladder?"

"Through the opening in your penis."

I shivered. I hadn't felt a thing.

Dr. Meyer pulled a blue Magic Marker from his pocket. "And now, my friend, we're going to have to shave your head and drill a couple of holes so we can secure the traction."

"Couldn't I just promise not to move my head?"

The doctor laughed. "I'm afraid that won't do, son."

A nurse shaved my head, then Dr. Meyer guided the Magic Marker across my scalp. It tickled! I giggled. Maybe sensation was beginning to return.

"Steve, this isn't going to hurt, but it's going to sound like all hell is breaking loose."

"You're sure you won't drill too far?"

"No, that's why we drew the—"

"What?"

The reverberation caused by metal on bone silenced me. The drill was a jackhammer, my skull a sidewalk. I tried to suck my brains down to my stomach.

After the drilling stopped, the doctor inserted metal rods into the holes—he called them tongs—and attached a wire that led to several gray weights.

Mom came in. She didn't show any emotion. She must have really hurried to the hospital. Her curly black hair wasn't brushed and her yellow blouse didn't match her brown slacks.

"Where's Dad?" I asked. Somehow, I felt, he should be able to straighten everything out.

"He's on his way. How do you feel?"

"Okay. Can you get Rensy here?"

"I'll try," Mom said.

"And call Bill, please?"

Bill Solomon had been my best friend since kindergarten. I knew he'd want to know what was going on.

The door opened. I saw my father before he saw me.

"Hi, Dad."

"Oh my God," my father said, and then he clutched his chest and dropped to the floor.

I screamed "Dad" and instinctively moved to help until I remembered I couldn't move. Dr. Meyer rushed across the room. In a minute my father was up.

"Just a little shock," said Dr. Meyer.

Dad straightened his suit, walked over to me, and took my hand. His shock wore off faster than mine was wearing off.

My memory of the rest of that first day is sketchy.

A nurse brought me a hamburger. Mom fed me, breaking the meat into digestible chunks, wiping the crumbs from my face.

Rensy came in with his mother. We had been friends for twelve years, ever since kindergarten. We were the first two boys in our class to read, and, I believe, the last two able to tie our shoes. We were hoping to go out East together for college—Rensy to Princeton and me to Harvard or Yale.

Renslow Drew Sherer was WASPy handsome, trim, with fair skin and light brown hair. Until he had lost forty pounds over the summer before freshman year, he was almost obese. Yet he had always been a fine, graceful athlete, and we had played sports together forever. I pitched while he manned first base for our grade school softball team. His father taught us how to play hockey on the outdoor rink by our elementary school (Rensy played goalie; I played center), and during the off season we perfected our skills with tennis balls and sticks wrapped in towels on the hardwood floor in the large studio where Rensy's mother taught dance. We went out for soccer together, me in the goal this time, Rensy at fullback. (After practice, we passed the time waiting for the bus to take us home by harmonizing on Beatles' songs.) Now we played a take-no-prisoners game of handball every Wednesday after school.

We were scheduled to play this day. Instead, he stood with

his mother by my hospital bed, his eyes red and swollen, his hands shaking.

"It's not your fault," I said. "Everything's going to be okay."

He didn't answer. He didn't look at me. He didn't leave his mother's side. Mrs. Sherer said goodbye for both of them.

My best friend Bill came in a few minutes after Rensy and his mom left. "I've called everyone I could think of," he said. "I'll help coordinate visits."

"I'm not going to be here that long," I said. "As soon as the shock wears off . . ."

Bill put his hand on my shoulder.

"I felt that," I said.

"I'll come tomorrow after practice." He had been the best athlete in our grade school class, and at six feet three now played basketball for rival New Trier West.

"We're still going to Second City for New Year's," I called out as he left.

"If you can get a date," he said with a smile.

I remember that there was only one other person in the Intensive Care Unit, a man named George. The nurse said that he had been in an auto accident and had thirteen fractures. He was in an oxygen tent. I couldn't see him, but I heard every labored breath he took. "I feel sorry for him," I told my parents. And then I must have finally fallen asleep.

·   ·   ·

Late in the afternoon, some eight hours after I had been brought to the hospital, Dr. Meyer shepherded my parents into a vacant office. "I don't know how much you know about the central nervous system," he began, "but the spinal cord is the pathway for the messages that the brain sends to the rest of the body. When that pathway is damaged, the messages simply don't get where they're supposed to go." He explained that the spinal cord was protected from head to torso by bones called vertebrae. "Unfortunately, when Steve hit the mat, his fifth cervical vertebra, that's the one about here," he said pointing to a spot at the back of his neck, "fractured and went into the spinal cord, in effect damaging the path so the messages can't get through. That's why he's paralyzed."

My mother pictured a bomb exploding in the Vietnam jungle. She wondered if the messages, like the industrious Viet Cong, could simply go around the blown-up pathway.

Neither she nor my father spoke, so Dr. Meyer forged ahead. "It's too early to tell if the damage and the paralysis are permanent. The cord is badly swollen from the trauma, and it will take about forty-eight hours for the swelling to subside enough so that we can even get an idea. Our concern right now is to keep Steve's vital signs stable. He can breathe on his own, but he doesn't have bowel or bladder control and he can't regulate his own body temperature. He's a sitting duck for infection or pneumonia."

My mother took a drag on her cigarette. "I want arrangements made so that I can sleep at the hospital."

Dr. Meyer stood up. "Mrs. Fiffer, you have no idea what a long haul you are in for. Steve's going to require at least two surgical procedures. You are going to need to sleep. You are going to need to eat. You are going to need to maintain some semblance of normalcy with your boys at home."

The doctor would later tell me, "Your mother is a formidable woman." This was old news. Mom had grown up in Marquette, Michigan, an Upper Peninsula town often featured as the coldest spot in the country. Winters were so bad that residents put their cars up on blocks in November and didn't take them down again until March. Mom could (and did) say with all honesty that when she was our age she walked several miles a day to school through blinding snowstorms.

She preached a similar gospel of self-reliance to her children. No rides to school on subzero days (unlike the "hothouse flowers," as she called those whose mothers drove them everywhere in the winter). And no cushy summer camp like the ones where most of our friends went to play softball and tennis—games they could play at home. My brother Jim and I went to Thunderbird, a canoe-tripping camp in Bemidji, Minnesota, for eight weeks each summer. By the time I was fourteen, I had gone on a twenty-one-day canoe trip in Canada's rugged Quetico country. We went for days without seeing anyone outside our party, and the trip featured numerous difficult, lengthy portages, including one of two miles.

Sam Rose, Mom's father, had owned the classiest haberdashery in Marquette. The family—one of only a few Jewish clans in town—was comfortable and cultured, frequently traveling to Chicago to take in theater and art exhibitions. Mom fell in love with the city and entered the University of Chicago in the mid-1940s. She lived in a women's co-op on campus, which apparently was very risqué for the times. The residents set their own rules, including men's visiting hours.

Unfortunately, she lasted only a year at the university. The school required undergraduates to take year-end exams that determined whether they passed on to the next year or failed. Mom thought she wrote one of the best tests of her life at the end of her freshman year. "I knew everything," she once told me.

That was the problem. Her professor—Norman MacLean, well known now as the author of *A River Runs Through It*—failed her because she wrote everything she knew (which, he acknowledged, was considerable) instead of answering the specific questions. Rather than repeat the year, she dropped out; said goodbye to my father, whom she had met and dated at the university; and headed to New York City and a career in the fashion industry.

She was living in the Barbizon Hotel for Women, apprenticing as a buyer for a department store, when Dad took the train there to ask her to come back to Chicago and marry him. She did and promptly went into the business of manufacturing leaders. (When I was in first grade, one of the older boys in the neighborhood told me to throw a tennis ball at a car motoring down our street. I did, squarely hitting the driver's side window. Mom saw the whole thing and ordered me inside. She was disturbed that I had endangered the driver by throwing the ball, but what really made her mad was the fact that I had let my neighbor tell me what to do. "Fiffers are leaders, not followers," she said. "Do you understand?" I did after that.)

After Dr. Meyer dissuaded her from spending that first night at the hospital, my mother went home as ordered, but did not sleep. As morning approached, she climbed out of bed and went across the hall to the room marked by a faux wood nameplate: STEVO. She harbored no illusion that her oldest child would be there, that this was all a bad dream.

The shades have not been pulled. The front light from the Egans' house across the street cuts a diamond on one wall, illuminating a row of debate and sports trophies. My mother closes the shades and curses the Egans. There are four little ones according to her latest count. A month earlier a delivery man had come to our door holding their youngest, two-year-old Johnny. "I almost ran him over. He was in the middle of the street," the shaken driver said. When Mom took Johnny home, Margaret Egan merely smiled and said, "I wonder how he got out."

Par for the course, my mother thinks. The young Egan kids learn to ride their bikes in the street, not on the sidewalk; they climb trees and jump down from dangerously high branches; they shoot darts and arrows at each other's heads. And none of them ever gets hurt.

"Not fair," my mother says out loud. She thinks about all the time she spent teaching me to look both ways, reminding me to fasten my seat belt. *I made sure he waited forty-five minutes after he ate before going swimming. I made him wear a helmet when he played hockey. For what? Goddamn Margaret Egan.*

She turns on the light in my room. On my bed rest the shoes and clothes I had worn to school less than twenty-four hours ago. She has no idea how they got there.

On my desk sit a pile of college catalogues and the partially completed applications to Harvard, Yale, and Stanford. She has no idea how I will ever be able to finish them.

She notices that one of the desk drawers is partially open, and she pulls it out. The drawer is filled with newspapers and school papers, jewelry boxes and cigar boxes. She begins emptying the contents on the floor, looking for some clue that will reveal the future confronting her, confronting us.

My coin collection. Newspaper clippings. Baseball autographs. A powder blue cuff-link box with two medals from my preteen speed-skating days. The first was silver—runner-up because I was too young to figure out that wide turns on an oval course are fatal. The second was gold; I had learned my lesson. But what of the third medal? She smiles. After apparently successfully defending my title, I was disqualified for diving across the finish line (solely for dramatic effect, I admitted). *These medals tell his story,* she thinks: *Innocence, Success, Cockiness.*

Deep in the drawer, she finds a pair of jockey shorts dyed green. I had worn them under green tights to preserve my respectability as Peter Pan in the sixth-grade play. On the morning of the first performance, after weeks of rehearsal, I had awakened with a fever of 102. I argued with the doctor for several minutes, finally persuading him to let me perform. I almost fainted when they put on my makeup, and chewed cough drops in between scenes. Our teacher-director, Mr. Martin, fanned me whenever I was offstage. I got a standing ovation, more for my courage than my acting ability. The next day I woke up covered with measles.

The underwear reminds my mother of another moment. Me at twelve—a nasty infected big toenail removed, instructions from the doctors to wear a moccasin and stay off the foot for two days. Home from the doctor's office, she had turned her back only to find me outside playing baseball—wearing one gym shoe and one moccasin. "I'm playing for the Indians," I told her.

He is a fighter.

When she came home from the hospital that evening, my mother told our cleaning lady, Willie Bee, what had happened to me. Willie Bee, six feet tall, 200 pounds, a formidable presence, stayed at our house two days a week. A superstitious woman, she believed her good luck would begin after she had buried her seventh husband; she had three to go. When she heard that I couldn't move, she started crying. "I ain't surprised," she said. "You all put too much stock in that boy."

Nonsense.

My mother walks to my closet. She removes a wooden box from the floor, then settles on my bed. She opens the box as if it contains buried treasure, then takes out a brush and a small metal container.

My father lumbers in, still half asleep. "What are you doing?" he asks, rubbing his eyes.

My mother doesn't look up. "Shining his shoes. I just know he's going to need them."

"Dear God, I hope so." He takes her hand.

"We can't let him know what the doctors said. We can't be weak in front of him," my mother says.

A conspiracy is born.

My mother applies the dark brown polish to the leather— rubbing, rubbing, rubbing, until she has become Aladdin, the shoe her magic lamp.

She knows what to wish for.

CHAPTER 2

In 3000 B.C., an unidentified Egyptian physician recorded
the first description of an injury to the spinal cord. After treating a man who had apparently fallen while working on a
building for the pharaoh, the doctor wrote, "Thou shouldst
say concerning him: One having a dislocation in the vertebra
of his neck while he is unconscious of his two legs and his two
arms and his urine dribbles. An ailment not to be treated."

As the critical forty-eight-hour window for recovery passed,
I remained unconscious of my arms and legs, my urine drib-
bling through the catheter, which I still could not feel. Months
later, I would learn that not only did my symptoms mirror
those observed in Egypt some five thousand years earlier; so,
too, did my doctors' prognoses. A room full of grim-faced pe-
diatricians, internists, radiologists, orthopedists, and neuro-
surgeons told my parents that mine was an ailment with no
hope of cure and little hope of improvement. My spinal cord
had not been severed, the doctors said, but it had been so
badly damaged that in all likelihood I would spend the rest of
my life in a wheelchair.

"It doesn't look good," said one neurosurgeon. "We'll be
able to stabilize his neck through surgery. He'll be able to turn

his head, but beyond that. . . ." He brought his hand to his forehead, blocking his eyes from view. "You know at this age they look like adults, but their bones are still the bones of children. Tiny." With luck, I might be able to control a battery-powered chair with my hands; if not, I could be taught to move the chair by puffing into a special tube.

I have recently read that when the spine and spinal cord are removed for autopsy, doctors reconstitute the human body with wood. "A broomstick is convenient," writes the noted British pathologist Trevor Hughes. "The sharpened lower end [is] thrust into the remains of the sacrum, whilst the upper end is inserted through the foramen magnum. Finally a cross-piece of wood is placed across the shoulders and the wood-frame covered with cotton waste or plaster of Paris."

If you are a religious person, you might find the body robbed of its spinal cord a symbol of the crucifixion. If you are more cynical, you might find it a scarecrow. In the days following the accident, our family friends seemed to consider me a combination of the two. Few of these well-meaning individuals knew anything about my type of injury save that a person meeting the hangman dies from a broken neck. Thus, after expressing their sympathy and surprise that I was alive, they politely asked my parents if I could still talk or think.

I could do both, of course, and at the same time! And even though I couldn't wiggle a toe or wag a finger, I quickly found that I could move—albeit in a most unconventional and unexplainable manner. By floating.

Floating. In the days following the accident, I often felt as if I weren't in my body. I could rise to the top of the room and look down at everything: at myself and at all the activity surrounding me. Up on the ceiling, I didn't pass judgment on what was going on below or come to any heavy conclusions about how I or anyone else was reacting to this "traumatic event." I just observed—like a camera without a photographer or, and maybe this is more accurate, like a dog observes. The accident had fractured more than my fifth cervical vertebra, broken more than my neck. It had fractured reality, broken time.

Christmas Eve 1967. I look at myself as I might look at a painting. I am: *Still Life of a Human Being.* In the nineteen days I have been in the hospital, my dark brown hair has begun to grow back, but my head still looks pretty mangy. From my scalp, the traction rods rise like the twin towers of Chicago's Marina City. My face looks thinner and it's badly broken out. I haven't shaved—or rather, been shaved—but my beard is barely visible. My arms have dwindled something terrible; the plastic identification band which was fastened tightly around my wrist when I was admitted now hangs loosely. A green foam padding has been wrapped around my elbows to prevent bedsores and more of the same material cushions my rear end. Nevertheless, a half-dollar-sized, prune-colored sore now graces my right buttock. My pubic hair has been shaved and the catheter still extends to a bag at the side of the bed. Although my thighs still look pretty strong, my calves have really shrunk. There's more foam under my heels. My feet look even paler than the rest of my body, and there is a pink-blue delta on each instep where the tributaries of various veins seem to converge.

Today, for the first time, I see my new scars. A long jagged pink line runs diagonally from right hip to thigh. This must be where they took the bone that they put into my neck. (Is this possible? *The hipbone connected to the neckbone?*) The operation is called an anterior fusion because they go in from the front. In my case, they removed the broken fifth cervical vertebra (C-5), then used a mallet-type surgical instrument to gently, slowly (micromillimeter by micromillimeter, the doctor said) tap in a replacement shaped from a slab of hip. They then wired this mock fifth vertebra to C-4 above and C-6 below.

The surgeon has left his signature not only on my hip, but across the entry point for the operation—my throat. The scar there looks like a four-inch paper cut. These two new scars join one that is now ten days old—this on the back of my neck from a laminectomy—an operation to remove as much damaged bone from the cord as possible.

Apparently, they've been doing laminectomies for years, but the anterior fusion is a new and improved way of giving stability to the head after an accident like mine. These operations were done from the back of the neck until the surgeons treating the wounded in Vietnam figured that a frontal maneuver would cause less additional damage to the spinal cord. (It's the trauma-shattered bone slicing into the spinal cord that causes the paralysis in the first place.)

My father had approached my injury as he would approach a complex lawsuit or transaction—by finding and reading everything written on the subject. Thus, when Dr. Meyer said that he had never performed an anterior fusion, Dad not only was familiar with the procedure, he knew where to find someone who had performed the operation. Indeed, he knew where to call one of the orthopedic surgeons who had pioneered the fusion; Dr. Wayne Southwick was in New Haven, Connecticut, practicing medicine and teaching at Yale.

Southwick was too busy to come, but his protégé, Dr.

Kristaps Keggi, was available. The doctor took pictures throughout the procedure. Someday my neck may be famous. After I woke up following the fusion, Dr. Keggi asked me to say something, anything. "Why?" I asked, or rather, whispered; my throat felt as if it had been sandpapered.

He explained that during the operation it had been necessary to temporarily move my vocal cords to gain access to the spine. "Some patients lose the ability to talk," he said.

I could talk, but I was in such pain that the doctor prescribed morphine. That night my parents looked green to me—the color of the Wicked Witch in *The Wizard of Oz*. After they left, I thought I saw a heavyset man with a dark mustache hovering over my bed. "I'm Dr. White," the man said. He was real.

I didn't respond. I was having trouble breathing—a state of affairs that had led the night nurse to summon this Emergency Room doctor to my private room.

"Your lungs are congested because of the operation, and your diaphragm isn't working well enough to cough up the fluid," explained Dr. White. He showed me a tube like the one my dentist sticks in my mouth to suck out spit and water—except it was as long as the rod a plumber sticks down the toilet when it gets clogged.

"Let's see if this works," he said, snaking his would-be divining rod past my tongue, gagging me. "Hurts," I gasped, but he kept going. My chest heaved. "Sick," I tried to say, but he still kept going. I spit out the tube the way a fish spits out a lure. Unfortunately, I was still breathing—or not breathing— about as well as a fish on land.

"Your throat is too sore from the surgery," Dr. White explained. "I've got another idea." And with that, he climbed onto my bed and sat on my stomach! Gagging again, I told my arms to wake up and throw this idiot off of me. I gasped. My arms weren't listening. I heaved. Bulls-eye! The phlegm hit my tormentor on the chin before he jerked his head away.

Dismounting, Dr. White wiped his face with *my* clean washrag. "Are you okay now?" he asked.

I took a deep breath. "Yes. Thank you."

"Sometimes we must resort to the unorthodox."

I floated to the ceiling after that. And now, two days later, breathing better and morphine-free, I'm back up here, watching the nurses take off my covers. I now live on a very narrow mattress bolted to two huge metal circles that run on each side of me from the head of the bed to its foot. Five gray weights—four 5-pounders and one 3-pounder—are suspended behind the head of the bed. They are hooked to the wire running from the rods in my scalp and remind me of the cans you see on the cars of couples JUST MARRIED. Traction.

Because the traction keeps my head back, I'm forced to look up at the ceiling. Dad came up with the idea of running a metal bar between the circles at their high point a few feet above my head. The bar supports a six-inch television set. At first I also had a watch on the bar, but it got too frustrating at night. I would fall asleep, then wake up thinking I'd been out for a couple of hours only to see that the minute hand had barely moved. I'd rather not know.

There is one more piece to the bed. A padded board, the same length and width as the mattress, rests in the corner by the window until it is needed. I'm a sitting duck for bedsores, so it's important to get off my backside. The nurses don't want to turn me manually, so they put the board, which has an extra opening for the eyes and extra padding for the forehead and chin, on top of me. Then they bolt the board to the mattress beneath.

I watch this turning procedure now from my spot on the ceiling. I look like a sandwich with toothpicks that keep the bread from falling apart, to keep the meat in the middle. When the toothpick-bolts are secure, a nurse presses a button. The bed's circles begin rotating. The mattress rises. Forty-five degrees, ninety degrees, then all the way over until I'm face down, the floor my new vista.

The bolts are unfastened The mattress (once underneath me) is removed from its new position above me. My naked rear end breathes.

The special bed leaves room for little else. A couple of gray chairs for visitors. A portable table. A speakerphone. A pitcher of water, as I'm supposed to drink as much as possible to prevent bladder infection. There's also a bowl of applesauce to help the pills go down. After having never been able to swallow capsules, I had just mastered the art before I got hurt. Now, stuck on my back, I can't do it.

My mother has taped a large poster to the wall by the foot of the bed—a drawing of Peter Pan sent by my former teacher Marvin Martin's sixth-grade class. When Mr. Martin heard about my accident, he wrote warm letters to both me and Rensy (who had played Smee). Then he canceled rehearsals for this year's production, *The Adventures of Tom Sawyer,* and announced the revival of *Peter Pan,* "in Steve's memory." Memory sounded a bit ominous. Wasn't that for dead people?

There's an eight-track tape deck on a metal shelf by the bathroom door. So far I only have one tape—something by Dionne Warwick—but I'm expecting more for Christmas. When I grow tired of Dionne asking if I "know the way to San

," I can listen to a cassette Bill Solomon made for me right
.ter the accident. He put his tape recorder next to his radio
one night and captured the WLS Top 40 Countdown in its en-
tirety. I've listened to the number-one song, "Incense and Pep-
permints," by Strawberry Alarm Clock, a dozen times already,
and I still have no idea what it's about.

A small gray table full of get-well cards sits by the window.
These cards are sent directly to the hospital now, not home.
Because my arms remain paralyzed, I can't open or hold the
mail. My friend Bob Luskin does this for me when he comes
over on his lunch break from Highland Park High School, just
a few minutes away from the hospital.

Everett Dirksen, Illinois's Republican U.S. senator, has sent
wishes for a speedy recovery and a note saying that he is going
to put something in the *Congressional Record* about me. We
have no idea how he heard about the accident. "Nice gesture,
but he's still not gonna get my vote," Dad said.

One of Dad's clients has sent something called a novena. I
had no idea what this was until a nurse explained that the
client had made a contribution to the church so that a priest
would pray for me. Since our rabbi had been in a few days earlier, I figured all bases were now covered.

There's also a huge get-well card featuring Snoopy. It was
signed by about a hundred of my classmates. Luskin (he never
answers to Bob) read every signature to me. I'd perked up
when he mentioned Carrie Baker, a senior whom I wished
would have paid attention to me when I sat next to her in U.S.
History. "Maybe I'll ask her out when I get back to school,"
I'd said to Bill during one of his visits, temporarily forgetting
that it would take several novenas before a girl that cool
would go out with me.

My favorite card features a drawing of a powder blue rabbit bandaged from head to toe. "Sorry to hear you went flippity-floppity," reads the front. Inside the card, a fully recovered bunny bounces merrily. "Hope that you soon will be hippity-hoppity." It hurts to laugh, but I couldn't stop when Luskin showed this one to me. This is all so absurd.

I met Luskin, a slight and owlish-looking seventeen-year-old, six months ago, when we were Cherubs—the odd (and inappropriate) name given to the cocky teenagers from around the country selected to participate in a five-week summer institute in debate, film, theater, journalism, or business at Northwestern University in Evanston. He and I were debate partners.

Mom and Dad had decided that debate was my ticket to the Ivy League. I'd debated with them all my life, so they probably knew what they were talking about. But because the forensics team met after school, I had to choose between it and soccer my junior year.

"You were very mature and made the right choice," Mom said.

That's debatable. I preferred to define myself in athletic terms rather than academic ones, and the girls I was interested in were more attracted to guys carrying cleats than those toting file boxes.

Although I was elected captain of the team, I was aware that several debaters didn't like me. They charged that I was a lazy researcher who won only because I was quick on my feet. I pled guilty, although I didn't understand what the crime was. As long as you're honest, who cares how you win?

Because Luskin was also lazy and quick, we spent much less time in the library than most of the other Cherub debate teams.

Because he was also a smart aleck, we spent much more time in trouble than any other Cherubs. The topic for the year was: *Resolved: Congress should establish uniform procedures for criminal investigations.* Most teams developed cases based on the historical and pragmatic interpretation of the search-and-seizure provisions of the Fourth Amendment. We initially took a more literal approach, proposing that investigators wear particular uniforms while conducting their investigations. Despite our explanation that we would be able to catch opponents off guard by quoting Mr. Blackwell instead of Sir Blackstone, our coach was not amused.

I didn't care. I had fallen hard for a cute southerner in the theater program, wooing her away from a California surfer type who had actually been a contestant on *The Dating Game.* The good news was: Pat and I spent almost every night making out on the Lake Michigan beach. The bad news was: I missed bed check so many times that I was assigned to clean the dormitory bathroom on weekends.

"I hope you're getting laid," said my roommate, another surfer, as I woke early one Sunday morning to scrub toilets.

I wasn't. Pat and I spent all our time above each other's waists. She said she wasn't ready for anything more. "Stop. I'm a good Jewish girl," she protested whenever I attempted to search and seize without a warrant.

"I'm a good Jewish boy," I said. But she won that debate every time.

After the accident, one of my friends said that if I had stayed with soccer instead of debate, I wouldn't have been in wrestling class the day I was hurt. The varsity athletes had a separate gym period at the end of the day. I didn't respond, but I started thinking about that and a lot of other what-ifs.

I had always prided myself on the fact that I never got sick. What if for once in my life I'd been home with the flu that day like my brothers and so many of my classmates?

What if I had paired up with someone besides Rensy?

What if Rensy and I had started wrestling five seconds after Mr. Hurley blew the whistle instead of right away? Or if we'd have started on a different spot on the mat? Or if I'd have managed to free a hand before falling? Would I have avoided catastrophe?

Maybe. But maybe if this accident hadn't happened, something else might have, something even worse. Maybe I'd have been hit by a stray bullet outside the stadium the next time I went to a Bulls game. Maybe I'd have been electrocuted in the bathtub. Maybe Dad would have been in a car crash on the expressway instead of being at the hospital visiting me. Maybe I'd have been the one standing over Rensy instead of vice versa.

I am up on the ceiling trying not to think about this when my special speakerphone rings. A nurse presses the ON button for me. I hope it isn't another reporter. Last week someone from our local weekly newspaper called. My mother was in the room. After asking several questions about my family and school activities, the reporter asked if I would ever walk again.

The question surprised me. "Of course," I said. No one had ever suggested to me that I wouldn't.

Mom was already heading for the phone when the next question came, "Steve, how does it feel to have a broken neck?"

"Broken neck?" I looked at Mom for guidance. I knew nothing about a broken neck.

"What kind of question is that? Who is your superior? I'll

have your job," Mom bellowed at the speaker before pounding the OFF button. "The nerve," she said to me.

"Do I have a broken neck? I thought I had a fractured cervical vertebra."

"It's the same thing, honey. You have a broken vertebra in your neck."

I was silent for quite a while, wishing I had paid attention during biology class. "Somehow 'broken neck' sounds a lot worse," I finally replied.

Mom nodded and put her hand on mine. "I know. That's why we haven't used it."

"I *am* going to be okay, aren't I?"

"Of course."

The doctors seem just as optimistic. They tell me that it just takes the spinal cord a long time to heal and that the bone banged into mine pretty hard when I hit the mat. I believe them, but for some reason whenever I hear them talking about me in the hall, I whistle so that I can't hear what they're saying.

Whistling is about all I can do. My hands don't work. My fingers don't work. My legs don't work. And neither does my penis.

My body is written in a foreign language that I can't translate. I am helpless. Totally dependent for survival on doctors, nurses, family, friends. The other day the mother of one of my father's young law partners—a buxom, dyed-blond princess in her sixties—was at the hospital to pay a call on her sister and poked her head in.

"This is why I never allowed my children to participate in sports," she said, adding, "How terrible. You can't even pick your nose."

Or scratch my head or wipe my ass or beat off.

The voice on the speakerphone this time belongs to the volunteer at the Visitors' Desk. She announces that Dave Scott, a classmate who works on the yearbook, is waiting to see me. I'm editor-in-chief, and he's brought me some copy to approve.

"He can come up," I say.

I don't like Dave very much. He transferred from another high school at the beginning of the year and marched into the office demanding to be coeditor-in-chief. Right! As if I hadn't worked hard for the job.

Juniors normally serve as assistants to the editors. Last year, however, one of the senior copy editors was asked to leave, and I had taken his place. In the spring, our faculty adviser, Mr. Frey, who made the senior-year staff assignments, asked me what editorships I was going to apply for. "Editor-in-chief," I said.

"What's your second choice?"

"I don't have a second choice. Editor-in-chief is all I'm interested in. I've earned it."

This is Dave Scott's first visit. What a shock it must be to see me flipped on my stomach, bare butt looking at the ceiling, eyes on the floor. He positions himself so I can see him from the knees down and says, "Hi, Steve. I was on my way to a party up this way, so I thought I'd drop off these articles and tell you things are going well back at the office." His voice is as high-pitched and annoying as ever. He explains that with Mr. Frey's consent he has instituted some organizational changes.

I've seen *All About Eve* on *The Late Show* twice. This asshole wants my job. Not without a fight.

"Who are you?" I ask.

"Oh, I'm sorry. It's me. Dave Scott."

"The name, the name, the name is familiar," I say, stifling a laugh, "but the face, the face, the face."

He bends down to show me his fat round face.

Again. "The name, the name—" then very dramatically: "Those things on your feet, are those . . . are those *shoes?*"

"Yes."

Dave thinks he is witnessing a major breakthrough.

"And those things under your shoes, are those *socks?*"

"Yes. Socks."

"And those blue things—pants?"

"Yes. Pants."

"Hi, Dave." I say it suddenly, but matter-of-factly, catching him completely off guard.

"Are you okay?" he asks.

"Sure. Why?"

"It's just all that talk about shoes and socks."

"What talk?"

"You know. You asked me if I were wearing shoes and socks."

"Why wouldn't you be? It's the middle of winter."

"I think I'd better be going."

Indeed.

I wish he could see the smile on my face. I can see the terror in his eyes, because even though my body is facedown, I'm back on the ceiling. Floating. Free.

Maybe I'm not as helpless as I thought.

CHAPTER 3

Moving quickly across the hospital parking lot, a shopping bag full of gifts in tow, my father passed one of the nurses from my floor.

"Morning, Santa," the young woman said with a smile.

Sans bag, Robert Fiffer would hardly have been mistaken for Santa Claus on this Christmas morning. He was darkly Semitic. His hair, thinning a bit on the top, was jet black, as were his eyebrows, which almost ran together, a furry furrow creating the impression that he was deep in thought. And he usually was. Growing up on Chicago's West Side in the 1930s, one either became a hood or an intellectual; he had opted for the latter, despite, or perhaps because of, his own parents' lack of schooling and money.

My grandfather had operated a corner hamburger grill. The family lived in two rooms behind the storefront. The story goes that they were so poor that they kept all their money in a bowl of lettuce in the icebox.

The family was poor because of the Depression and because my grandfather was a dreamer who spent much of his time trying to break into the songwriting business. He had actually collaborated with the bandleader Lawrence Welk for a while—unfortunately, long before Welk made it big. When Grandpa Fiffer died in 1954, none of his songs had ever been recorded, not even my favorite, "My In-laws Made an Outlaw Out of Me."

My father had little time to dream. He had always been a man in a hurry. At fifteen, he graduated from high school and began commuting by el train to the University of Chicago. By the time he was twenty, he had earned both his undergraduate and law degrees from the university and was helping to support his parents. He quickly passed the bar exam, but had to wait until he was twenty-one before he could be admitted to the practice. He was twenty-one when he married my mother and twenty-three when I was born in 1950.

My mother says that Dad told her not to let my younger brother Jim and me bother him until we had read the Great Books. In the meantime, he was working nights and weekends to build a law practice. Many of the bigger firms in town would not employ Jews, so he joined a father-and-son operation, Cohen & Cohen. Eventually, it became Cohen, Cohen & Fiffer as Dad parlayed his work for one Democratic state legislator into an extensive network of contacts with the Cook County Democratic machine and appointments to the State Fair Employment Practices Commission and Human Relations Commission. He thus attracted numerous clients who felt a lawyer's political connections were more important than his religious affiliation.

Dad kept a file box with the name of each of his contacts in city and county government and the judicial system. These relationships had to be nurtured constantly (and remembered with steaks or wine at Christmas). When his contemporaries at the blue-blood firms were burning the midnight oil researching the fine points of antitrust or securities law, Dad was eating chicken à la king at dinners for local officials or drinking gin with them at wakes for their political brethren. When I was ten, he took me to a $100-a-plate fundraiser for Mayor Daley. After he left our table and went to the bathroom for the third time, I asked if he was feeling all right. He said he was fine, that the reason he kept getting up was so that everyone would see that he was there.

They did, and with their help, Dad developed a reputation as a lawyer who knew how to fix things. Not parking tickets. Unbeknownst to clients and friends who asked him to make these go away, my father never cashed in favors at Traffic Court. Rather, he payed the fines out of his own pocket. "It takes too long to go over to court and talk to the right people," he explained to me. "If you put a couple of singles in the envelope and mail it in, the clerk who gets it takes care of it no matter who you are."

"Why don't you just tell your clients to do that?" I asked.

"Because this way I'm not only doing them a favor, I'm impressing them with my so-called connections."

The firm did utilize its connections at the county assessor's office, the agency responsible for property taxes. Most of the prestigious firms in town didn't have these contacts and felt it beneath their station or dignity to develop them. As a result, these firms referred to Dad those corporate and individual clients seeking reductions in their assessments. He was happy to take these referrals for many reasons: their fees kept the firm in the black, and, equally important, he reasoned that if he did a good job for them in this one area of the law, they might seek his representation on other matters. Similarly, bigger firms impressed by his small firm's work, might also refer other business. This is exactly what happened, and over the years Cohen, Cohen & Fiffer expanded its scope and clientele to become a well-regarded, all-purpose firm.

I watched the transition from a front row seat. In December 1955, we moved from a two-bedroom apartment in Chicago's South Shore neighborhood to a modest four-bedroom brick colonial in Glencoe, a North Shore suburb about forty-five minutes from the city. Dad immediately joined a local bowling league so he could get to know our neighbors and, perhaps, come to represent them. I tagged along to the Strike 'N Spare on Thursdays as mascot and, when I got a little older, team scorer.

As time went on, the events to which I was taken got classier, the milieus more dignified: State of Illinois Building meetings of the Human Relations Commission on which my father served. Courtrooms in the Cook County courthouse where his friends sat on the bench and sometimes embarrassed (and delighted) me by beckoning me to sit by them while court was in session. The courtroom at the University of Chicago Law School where, as a prominent alumnus, Dad played judge for the annual moot court competition.

Two nights before my accident, my father took me to another political dinner—this one for Mike Howlett, Illinois's secretary of state. Dad was Howlett's personal lawyer and political adviser and, not surprisingly, received a good deal of legal work from the secretary of state's office. Howlett had also found me a summer job in the city housing department and, more important, had once arranged for me to get my picture taken with Yankees first baseman Moose Skowron, who worked for the State of Illinois during the off season.

The secretary was a rising political star, a contender for governor, many thought, and the hotel ballroom was filled. This time, Dad didn't have to get up to go to the bathroom to get noticed. He was on the dais as the master of ceremonies, introducing not only Howlett, the mayor, and other local luminaries, but the keynote speaker, U.S. Senator Stuart Symington from Missouri. After the speeches, Dad introduced me to the senator.

We didn't get home until well after midnight, but we were both wide awake, energized. Master of ceremonies. A U.S. senator. The kid from behind the hamburger joint had come a long way. I hadn't done anything to earn my place at the table; my life had been so much easier than his. Where were my challenges going to come from? I wondered. What barriers was I going to have to overcome?

At school the next day, I couldn't stop talking about the evening. (I was so tired, my parents let me sleep in and miss the first two periods, including gym. What if I had slept in the following day, the day of the accident, instead?) I couldn't stop bragging about my dad, either.

But as much as I loved and respected and bragged about my father, I worked very hard during my teenage years to make his life miserable. I didn't fail any courses at New Trier. I didn't get in trouble with the law. I didn't get drunk or stoned or stay out all night or wreck the car or misbehave with the girls I dated. On the contrary, I made honor roll every semester, distinguished myself in extracurricular activities, didn't drink, get high, or even smoke a single cigarette. There were no late-night calls from the police, no girlfriend's father standing angrily on the doorstep. I did dent the door of Mom's Buick Electra pulling out of a parking space, but you couldn't even see the mark in the dark.

So how did I drive my father crazy? To use one of his words: I simply *ootzed* him to the breaking point.

A typical dinner at the Fiffers': Dad would arrive home from a taxing day at work and mix himself a Beefeater's martini; shortly after we'd sat down at the table, I'd insult Mom (a surefire way to annoy him); he'd warn me to stop; I'd intentionally do something seemingly innocuous, like "accidentally" dropping a fork; he'd explode and banish me to my room.

"For dropping a fork?" I'd ask.

"For dropping a fork?" Mom would echo.

I'd stomp off to my room. Although she was the original victim, Mom would tell Dad that he was being too hard on me; he'd protest for a minute, but then he'd call upstairs to me that I could come back to the table; through my closed door I would demand an apology before deigning to rejoin the family. And before too long, one of the city's best lawyers would throw in the towel. (All the years of watching him and others in court had apparently paid off.)

In a way, my chosen form of torture was more insidious than the standard teen rebellion. Because my public persona appeared so exemplary, my father could hardly complain to anyone about my behavior. Ootzing seemed so petty compared to boozing or playing hooky or getting stoned.

After one father-and-son battle, Mom told me that the house wasn't big enough for both my ego and Dad's. She wasn't amused when I replied by suggesting that we get a bigger house. In the hospital now, our world was considerably smaller than it had been at home, but despite this, or perhaps because of this, my father and I had not clashed since the accident.

A creature of habit, Dad arrived at the hospital every morning—weekday, weekend, or holiday—at seven-fifteen. Entering the hospital through the Emergency Room on this Christmas Day, he now climbed the single flight to 2 West. A "Good morning" from behind halted his journey. It was Sy Marmon, a surgeon with whom he served on the town caucus.

Dr. Marmon reported that he had run into the director of the Rehabilitation Institute of Chicago at a party. "I think you should talk to him, Bob. The institute does marvelous things for quadriplegics."

Quadriplegic. The word dizzied him. It was the first time he had heard it applied to me. Maybe some parents had quadriplegics, but not him; he had a seventeen-year-old son who couldn't move for the time being because he had broken his neck wrestling three weeks ago. Until now, there had seemed to be a difference.

My father caught his breath, shifted his bag of gifts from one arm to the other, and continued to my room. My mother had always celebrated Christmas in Marquette and had persuaded Dad that Christmas tree and Hanukkah menorah could coexist in our home. We exchanged presents on both holidays.

This year, however, Hanukkah had fallen victim to bad timing, coinciding with my first days in the hospital. And although we still had little to cheer about, my parents determined to make the most of December 25. Bill Solomon, who came every day, had helped by stealing a cardboard Santa from the Solarium and taping it to the inside of my door.

"Merry Christmas, Slugger," my father said as he entered my room. "And Merry Christmas to you, Miss Masters." Masters, my private day nurse, had just finished bathing me.

She was a small, officious woman in her early thirties with short brown hair, chalk white skin, and a perpetual frown.

My father handed her the present my mother had insisted that we give her. "That wasn't necessary," said Masters. She put the unopened package in the closet. Then she drained my urine bag.

"Maybe we should have just wrapped that for her," my father whispered to me.

I smiled.

He kissed me on the forehead, then opened the *Chicago Sun-Times*.

Ever since the day I began reading, Dad had been clipping articles of all sorts and leaving them on my pillow with a note: "Let's discuss." TRB's column in the *New Republic*. Roger Angell in the *New Yorker*. Everything and anything about the coming computer age. ("If you don't know Fortran, you'll be left behind," he warned me, referring to the language of computers). Once he left Martin Luther King, Jr.'s *Letter from a Birmingham Jail* with a note calling it the finest piece of writing he'd read in years. "Please let's discuss," the note begged.

I read the book, as I read most of the articles, but I rarely admitted that to him and hardly ever gave him the satisfaction of a discussion. I can't explain this immature behavior any more than I can understand my own kids' refusals to read the offerings I place on their pillows. (Roger Angell in the *New Yorker*. A *Time* magazine piece on "the language of computers." The TRB column in the *New Republic*).

In the hospital, because my hands weren't working and I couldn't hold a newspaper, Dad read the *Sun-Times* to me every morning. I was happy to discuss whatever he wanted, anything to get my mind off me and my future.

We always started with the sports section. My father had played the violin as a child, not baseball or football, but he was an avid sports fan and a fairly good athlete. He had never had the advantage of tennis lessons as a child, as I had. Indeed, I had never known him to even play the game. Yet, when I, at age ten, had challenged him to a match, he had shocked (and silenced) me by beating me soundly.

He had in recent years forsaken bowling for golf, taking the lessons he could never have dreamed of as a youngster. I, too, had taken lessons, and we brought our clubs along on most vacations. I could hold my own against him on the course, but I couldn't hold my temper. The past two summers, my friend Bill accompanied our family on end-of-August-bargain-rate vacations to the Diplomat Hotel in Florida. During one golf match, I had only to three-putt from fifteen feet to break 50 for the back nine on the resort's demanding main course. I four-putted. Driving the cart back to the clubhouse, I thought I heard Bill snicker. I elbowed him out of the moving cart. My father wouldn't play with me for the rest of the vacation.

We did better together as spectators. If the right seller was manning window number three, Dad knew the magic words to get great seats at Cubs games. "Richie Berkson," he'd say, invoking the name of a mutual friend, and we'd suddenly have tickets a few rows behind the dugout.

Even though the hated White Sox broke my heart and the Yankees' string of pennants in 1959, I had no qualms about going to game one of the World Series at Comiskey Park. Dad coaxed two tickets from a client whom we later discovered had mob friends if not mob duties. One ticket was in the third row behind the Sox dugout. The other was in the very last row of the grandstand. Dad stuck me in the box seat and trekked up to the nosebleed section. Just nine years old, I lasted only one inning by myself. The fellow sitting next to Dad with whom we traded tickets looked as if he'd been asked to sit in the dugout itself.

By the time of my accident, the Yankees' glory days were past. In 1967, the team had finished ninth in the American League, beating out only the Kansas City Athletics. To prolong his career and save his legs for life after baseball, the aging Mickey Mantle—all of thirty-five—had moved from the outfield to a more sedentary life at first base. He would play only one more season. Meanwhile, the White Sox, Red Sox, Twins, and Tigers battled for the pennant until the last week of the season before the Red Sox won. This sad state of affairs was driven home to me as my father and I flew to Boston in the middle of the World Series to begin our tour of colleges that interested me—Harvard, Amherst, Yale, and Princeton. As the Red Sox had not won a pennant since 1946, a World Series since 1918, all of New England was paralyzed by baseball fever.

Paralyzed. Long after I was out of the hospital, I learned that my father was more than bedside reader; he was censor and rewrite man, too. When reading the sports section, he omitted articles about injured players. He altered phrases. A team was never "crippled" by a player's absence; it was "hindered." A basketball player never "paralyzed" his man with a move to the hoop; he "froze" him.

On Christmas Day 1967, the Rose Bowl was in the news. Midway through an article about the upcoming game between Southern Cal and Indiana, there was a knock on my door. My father got up to answer it.

In the entranceway stood Lou and Laura Rossi, another

couple with a child in the hospital. Their daughter Susie lay in a room down the hall. She had encephalitis and was in a coma for the time being. The Rossis and my parents had met in the Solarium. Lou Rossi, a short, bald man in his fifties, and Laura, ten years younger and six inches taller, looked in on me regularly, and my mom and dad visited Susie's room each day.

"Merry Christmas," Dad said. "Any change with Susie?"

My father saw that Lou was trembling. "Susie died last night, Bob."

The newspaper fell from his hands. "Oh God. I'm sorry, Lou." The Fiffers and the Rossis had become partners in waiting. They had even talked about fixing their kids up when this was all over.

"We went home early this morning, but we couldn't sleep," Lou said quietly. "We had this present for Steve . . . and . . . well . . . Merry Christmas, son."

I opened my mouth. All that came out were tears. The Rossis left.

I kept crying, the first time I'd allowed myself to betray any emotion in front of anyone since the accident. "I can't believe they came back," I sobbed. "They're so nice. Everyone's so nice. I'm such a burden. It would be better if I die, too."

My father didn't know what to do. As a boy, he had seen his own father, broken by the Depression, cry many times. By the time he was in high school, he had concluded that wealth was the key to survival and to some extent happiness. Make enough money and you and your family wouldn't have to worry about anything.

And now? He had earned enough money to have given his sons everything he had missed as a kid—summer camp, tennis lessons, vacations to New York City and Disneyland, their own bedrooms. The family was free from want. But, god-dammit, all the money in the world couldn't make his oldest son move. He could fix almost anything for his clients, but he couldn't fix me.

I'm as powerless as my father was, he thought.

He took a deep breath. He couldn't work a Christmas miracle; he could only be my dad. He dried my eyes, then picked up the newspaper. He put his hand over mine and began to read.

CHAPTER 4

References to what we now call the spinal cord can be found in the earliest religious writings. The Talmud warns the Israelites that unless they bow during their prayers, their spinal cords will turn into snakes seven years after death. The Bible's book of Ecclesiastes predicts an even worse fate for the living: ". . . ever the silver cord be loosed . . . then shall the dust return to the earth as it was."

Had my "silver cord" been loosed at the fifth cervical vertebra just thirty years earlier, my dust most likely would have returned to earth within a month or two from some complication—pneumonia, infected bedsores, or dysreflexia, a bowel or urinary tract blockage that can result in a stroke or heart attack. But, due in part to the large number of World War II and Vietnam soldiers with spinal cord injuries, doctors had dramatically intensified the study of the cord and fashioned responses to increase the length and quality of life of the injured. Still, though they understood how the cord worked, they did not know how to fix one broken like mine.

Today, a little more than thirty years after my accident, there is for the first time serious talk of a cure for damage to the spinal cord. A seventeen-year-old high school student paralyzed in a wrestling accident in 1999 would be treated significantly differently than I was. Paramedics would rush him to a trauma center prepared to handle such injuries. There, doctors would immediately inject him with methylprednisolone, a steroid that reduces swelling of the spinal cord and damage to nerve cells.

In 1967, the greatest gift my doctors could give me was hope. "Am I really going to be okay?" I asked Dr. Meyer and any other doctor or nurse who came into my hospital room.

"Of course," came the stock answer. "These things just take time." The hospital staff, I realized much later, had its own conspiracy going.

By New Year's Eve, my right side remained dormant, but I had regained a small amount of motion in my left arm and wrist, and I could wiggle a finger or two on my left hand. (I was left-handed, but the doctors said that had nothing to do with the left side coming back first.) I took each new flutter as a sign that by the time the traction tongs in my head came out in late January, I would be walking again—this despite the fact that there was no sign of life below my waist.

I didn't make it to Second City with Bill to ring in 1968. But when he came to the hospital before going out that night, I reminded him that we were going to Florida over spring break. We had made those plans a few weeks before the accident. "I may not water-ski when we're down there," I said earnestly. "I wouldn't want to do anything that might screw up my fusion."

Just as earnestly, he said he understood.

After I was out of the hospital, Bill confided to me that his uncle, an orthopedist, had been among the first to look at my X-rays and had told him that the chances were slim that I would ever walk again, much less water-ski. Every time I brought up plans for some future activity, Bill had to respond from his heart (which hoped I would recover) instead of his head (which told him I probably would not).

My heart was controlling my intelligence as well. I truly believed that I would be going to Florida in the spring, and there was no doubt in my mind that I was going off to Harvard, Yale, or Stanford in the fall, assuming one of them found me worthy of admission. After all the trouble I'd just gone through completing their applications, I figured one of them damn well better admit me.

A few days after Christmas, Dad had pulled a chair over to my bed and said he wasn't getting up until I'd written my college essays. "I can't write," I said, stating the obvious.

"You dictate. I'll write," he said, brandishing pen and paper.

I had never dictated a letter, much less a five-hundred-word essay. I can remember the accident, the drilling of the holes in my skull, the night Dr. White had to sit on my stomach, but I have no recollection of the three hours that followed my father's dictatorial stance; the memory of "writing" the essays is simply too painful to recall.

My mind may have been playing tricks on me when I looked into the future and saw myself as I was before the accident, but my eyes were brutally honest about the present. Although the traction immobilized my head, locking my gaze upon the ceiling, I could see for myself that there was no movement from my waist down. A classmate who had broken his neck a few years earlier in a diving accident but had suffered no paralysis (lucky dog!) had brought me a special pair of glasses that he had worn while in traction. The glasses featured prism lenses that allowed me to see the foot of the bed.

Without the glasses, I could see only fragments of my friends and family—an elbow here, a nose there, a knee, a torso if I was lucky. A cubist's vision of my visitors. But now I could see the visitors stationed at the end of the bed, and, more important, I could see my toes.

Eddie Elisberg, my parents' internist, had told them that if (or, as they told me, *when*) movement returned below the waist it would begin with the big toe. Through my glasses I watched, wiggled (that is, tried to wiggle) and waited. Nothing. My stubborn toes refused to accept the charges from my brain.

And then, five weeks to the day after I had been hurt, I wiggled my toe. Or at least thought I wiggled my toe—the big one on my left foot. It was about 9 A.M. I said to myself as I always did, "You're going to move it today." Then I concentrated on how to make the toe wiggle (hard to believe it actually required concentration to figure out how to send such a simple message no more than six feet). And then I executed the wiggle itself. There was, I thought, a definite twitch.

My mother thought she saw something, too. "Was that a spasm?" she asked.

"I don't think so," I said, my heart pounding. The spasms made the entire foot fly or snapped my legs up to my chest. Most of the time they came without warning, and even if there was a warning, there was nothing I could do to stop them. This was different.

We needed a second opinion. Mom called in Nurse Masters. And again the toe wiggled. Or at least Mom and I thought it did. Masters wasn't sure. "I'm not ruling it out," she said. "Do it again." But I couldn't.

When Dr. Meyer came in about half an hour later, I dropped the bomb. "I wiggled my big left toe."

He said nothing as he picked up my hospital chart and began reading the nurses' notes. I couldn't fathom his nonchalance. Was he acting so casually because he thought that a wiggle of the toe was a perfectly logical thing for me to have done, or because he didn't believe me?

Maybe he just didn't hear me, I thought. "I wiggled my big left toe. Mom saw me."

"Steve." His tone answered my question. He sounded like my dad when I gave him a phony excuse for getting home late.

"You don't believe me."

"That's not true. I believe you *think* you moved it."

"I don't *think*. I *know*." I spoke to the doctor with an impatience reserved for my parents when I needed to release my anger about the present and fear about the future. "Here, I'll wiggle it again."

But I couldn't. The toe would not budge.

Masters was on break, but where the hell was my mother? She had gone to get coffee fifteen minutes ago. She should be back. If she were here, she'd tell him.

Meyer put his warm right hand on my shoulder as he always did, but said nothing.

My mother walked in as he was getting ready to go. "Tell him, Mom."

"He moved his toe, Roy."

"Walk me to the nurse's station, Elaine," said Dr. Meyer.

They walked silently to the Solarium, where the doctor motioned for my mother to sit on a high-backed blue chair by the snow-streaked window overlooking the hospital parking lot. As she took her seat, she noticed an ambulance move up the drive. She turned away. Meyer moved a chair directly in front of her.

"He really did wiggle his toe," my mother said.

"When are you going to face reality, Elaine. Your boy is never going to wiggle a toe or move a foot or stand or walk. He's going to be strapped into a wheelchair the rest of his life. Those are the cold, hard facts."

.   .   .

My mother had yet to return from her walk with Dr. Meyer when a voice came over the speaker that hooked me up to my classes. "Are you there, Steven? Come in, come in, Steven."

The voice belonged to Mr. Prince, my advanced placement English teacher. The two-way system over which he was speaking was connected from the high school to my room through the telephone lines. My speakerphone sat on a table several feet from the bed. If someone wasn't in the room to press the button down for me, I couldn't "come in."

"Steven. Come in, Steven."

"Steve told me to tell you that he'd be watching *Hollywood Squares* today and didn't want to be interrupted," said one of my friends. The class laughed. I would have laughed, too, except that Prince was pretty senile and was likely to believe that stuff. And senior English was the one remaining class I needed to graduate.

"Well, if you aren't watching television, Steven, why don't you grab a pencil and scan the lines while I read Hamlet's soliloquy."

"Grab a pencil!" I yelled at the speaker. "You old fart, if I could grab a pencil, I'd be in class."

Mom finally returned. As Prince approached the end of his overly dramatic rendition, I asked her to press the button. She gave me a dirty look, but obliged. "I'm here, Mr. Prince," I sang out, interrupting his performance. He never finished the speech.

When Miss Lennard, my Latin teacher, came on thirty minutes later and asked, "What's new?" I was tempted to go public with the toe-wiggling, but something stopped me. I just said, "Nothing much." Then she turned the speaker off at her end to give the class the latest medical bulletin about me—a bulletin delivered to her each morning by my friend and neighbor Billy Biederman, who was also in the class. Billy told me that she would give the report and then tell the class what a brilliant battle I was waging—just like Caesar's struggle with his detractors. I wasn't sure I liked the comparison, but I did like Miss Lennard. She was a gentle woman in her late fifties, unmarried, with the biggest bosoms I had ever seen. Some of us in the class called them Romulus and Remus.

After her daily paean, Miss Lennard turned the speaker back on and told me how thrilled my fellow students would be if I would translate the first paragraph of a new assignment. I didn't have the dexterity to write, but I could now hold a book or newspaper by myself by squeezing it in my left hand and balancing it on my chest. Mom found the page for me.

The guy who had sold me my Latin book had translated every page in the margins. It wasn't very difficult to oblige Miss Lennard. I had become adept at pretending to have the expected difficulty with a couple of the words each time I read. When I finished, the teacher seemed near tears.

Physical therapy followed English and Latin. Mr. Cole, head of the hospital's PT department, came in every day to take my legs and arms through the range of motion so they wouldn't be stiff when they started working again. I tried to wiggle my toe for him. Nothing.

"It will happen," my mother said before she went home to fix dinner for my brothers.

Late afternoon—before my parents and friends came back for the evening—was always the worst time for me. Alone, unable to distract myself, I would get to thinking. And there was little else to think about except me. Small things—the functioning of my bowels—could preoccupy me for several minutes. Bigger questions—exactly how much longer would this go on?—could tie me in knots for hours.

When I was alone, I often prayed out loud. The prayers were always neatly numbered. They were among the few aspects of my life in which I could maintain order.

1. *Please keep my parents alive and well.* (I lived in constant terror that my overweight father would drop dead from a heart attack or that my chain-smoking mother would be hospitalized with lung cancer. I knew I needed them both and couldn't imagine how I would carry on if either of them died or got sick.)

2. *Please end the war in Vietnam.*

3. *Please let me be whole again.*

I didn't want to be selfish, but after the first month I began thinking about reversing the order of the last two prayers.

When my parents returned after dinner that evening, my mother was fuming. "Do you know a gym teacher named Mr. Tilman?" she asked before even taking off her coat.

"Sure. Why?"

She explained that my brother Jim, a freshman, had come home from school close to tears. Today had marked the beginning of a new gym unit. Finding himself assigned to wrestling, in the same gymnasium in which I had been injured, Jim had quietly asked Mr. Tilman if he could participate in a different sport. Mr. Tilman responded by dressing him down in front of the entire class. "Would the wittle baby wike some cookies and milk, too?" the teacher had mocked. "Would he wike me to call his mommy?"

"It's been hard enough for him, and now this," my mother said.

I wished I could have done something. I had given Jim a lot of grief over the years, but I'd been the first to protect him when others tried to do the same. I had taught him how to hit a baseball, shoot a basket, lift a puck, kick a soccer ball, call a girl on the telephone, draw to the inside straight. I had included him with my friends in ball games and card games.

Our relationship could be summarized by a single event that took place in 1963, when I was thirteen and he was ten. The family went to McCormick Place for a closed-circuit broadcast of the NFL championship game between the Bears and the New York Giants (regular television coverage was blacked out in Chicago). While walking to the car after the game, Jim tripped over something—*Was it someone's foot?* he wondered as he fell face first in the snowy parking lot. He started to cry.

"You're going straight home, Steve," Dad said, even though we had dinner reservations at a restaurant in the Loop.

"Why?"

"Don't play dumb. I saw the whole thing. We'll drop you off and then the three of us will go out to dinner. Are you okay, Jim?"

"No," he said. His face hurt. So did the realization that his older brother had intentionally grounded him. He cried most of the way home.

"I'm really sorry, Jim," I said.

Silence.

"We've got a chance to make a point here," Dad whispered to Mom as he pulled the car into the driveway. "All we have to do is stick to our guns."

"I think I've learned my lesson," I implored. "Please, can't I go out with you?"

"No," mother and father said in unison. "Get out."

Jim finally broke his silence. "If Steve can't go to dinner, I don't want to go either."

Friends again, we played king of the hill on our exasperated parents' bed while they went out to dinner by themselves. Younger and smaller, Jim was roughed up worse than he had been in the parking lot; but this was, he knew, a good roughing up, not a mean-spirited one.

When I had been away at Camp Thunderbird for the first time in 1962, Jim, age eight, had reached an epiphany. "This is the first time I've ever been able to complete a sentence at the dinner table," he told my parents. Now, five years later, the accident had elevated him to my spokesperson. When my parents didn't feel like answering the phone and giving out the latest medical bulletin, they ceded responsibility to him.

The phone rang constantly, and the conversation was always the same. "How's Steve?" the callers asked. Then, "How are your Mom and Dad holding up?" Finally, they'd ask about our two-and-a-half-year-old brother, Tommy. Nobody asked how Jim was doing.

He wasn't always doing fine. Taking out the garbage a few days after Christmas, he had heard something pop in his lower back. Frightened, he then dropped the trash can on his foot. For the next few days, his pain was considerable, but it seemed too insignificant to mention. Finally, however, the injury hurt too much, and our Aunt Ruth took him from my room down to the Emergency Room. There, the doctor was unable to find anything wrong with back or toes.

"What did you say your name was?" the doctor asked.

"Jim Fiffer."

"Are you Steve's brother?"

"Yes."

The doctor turned to my aunt. "I think that explains it," he chuckled.

Talk about adding insult to injury.

I told my parents that Mr. Tilman was a prick and that they should report him to the dean of freshman boys or the head of the gym department.

Mom had brought me dinner leftovers—flank steak (already cut into manageable pieces) and mashed potatoes. Jim found the controls for the Circolectric bed and raised me to a suitable angle for dining. I reached for my fork awkwardly, like the claw that reaches for the grand prize in the carnival game. Fortunately, I didn't have to pay a quarter for every swipe until I grabbed the goods.

After dinner, my father stationed himself an inch from my big left toe, like a golfer trying to coax a putt that has stopped on the lip of the hole to drop in. No luck this time.

Later, my former girlfriend Randi stopped by for the third time in a week. She had been terrific throughout the past five weeks, feeding me milk shakes, reading to me. Sometimes late at night, she'd telephone, and we would talk past midnight about our families, college, future careers. I said I wanted to be a lawyer; she couldn't decide if she wanted to be a stewardess or a psychologist.

Tall, slim, and blond, Randi was one of the prettiest and most popular girls in the junior class. I hadn't had much luck with such girls in my class, but I'd known Randi for years and what began as a friendship slowly developed into . . . a friendship. We had gone out regularly, but not exclusively, with one another for several months and had not progressed beyond the kissing stage. I never pushed for more, because I'd heard that her father had almost knocked the head off of a boy whom he had found on the couch with his hand under Randi's sweater. I wasn't a particularly fast mover anyway, but when I did feel the longing to put my hand under a sweater, I called upon a couple of girls who were popular in a different way than Randi was.

I could live with the fact that I wasn't getting as far with Randi as my predecessor had and as many of my friends were getting with their girlfriends. Like most of my classmates, I believed popularity ranked only below class rank in order of importance. Dating someone considered cool wouldn't help your GPA, but it raised your social standing. It was as important to be "seen" at the high school as it was at the political fundraisers my father attended.

I made sure that I was seen with Randi. At New Trier, everyone was assigned to a student-supervised study hall for at least one period a day. As a freshman and sophomore, I had envied the study hall generals—juniors and seniors given free rein of the school to deliver and then pick up the study hall attendance charts for a particular period. These upperclassmen—well connected to the Student Council leaders responsible for appointing generals—often plucked their pretty girlfriends out of study hall to accompany them on their rounds. As a general my senior year, my first stop was always Randi's study hall. In the tradition of the great generals who had preceded me, I commanded my subordinate to discharge Randi for special assignment. Then I marched through the halls with my aide-de-camp/girlfriend at my side for all to see.

On the night before the accident, Randi and I had mutually agreed to stop going out. The split was so amicable that I wasn't surprised when she showed up at the hospital shortly after I was hurt. I also wasn't surprised that she had shown up with a friend. Visitors almost always came in twos the first time—paired like animals entering the Ark to ride out the anticipated flood of emotions unleashed by my pale stationary body and the foreboding bed, tubes, wires, and weights that made me look more like a construction site than a person. I was surprised, however, that Randi's partner was one of the girls with whom I had recently enjoyed a pleasant wrestling match on the living room couch without parental intervention; I didn't think they even knew each other.

Soon Randi started coming by herself. As we grew closer, I started thinking about her in a sexual way and wondered if she thought of me the same way. I could understand if she didn't. When she sat next to the bed, she could see the tube coming out from my crotch. Sometimes after she would leave, I'd try to get my hand down there to see if things were working, but the catheter and my limited range of motion conspired to frustrate my efforts.

Hours after I thought I had wiggled my toe, I tried to do it for Randi before she went home. No luck. As my parents prepared to leave, I tried again. Nope.

"It's like that riddle: if a tree falls in the forest and no one is there, has it made a sound?" I sighed. "If I wiggle my toe and nobody sees it, does that mean I haven't moved it?"

"Try again," Mom said as she buttoned her coat.

And I wiggled it! Unmistakably. Indubitably. Dammit all, I moved the bugger. This time I had two witnesses. My mother and father both thought they saw it, but just so there was no doubt, I did it again. And again.

Dad rushed to the vending machine and got as many cans of ginger ale as he could hold. Mom summoned Jim from the Solarium where he was doing his homework. We toasted my toe.

"Goddammit, you did it," Dad said. "You're gonna be okay."

"Was there ever any doubt?" I said confidently.

"Maybe just a little," he said.

"Never," said my mother.

.   .   .

When my mother had returned to the hospital after dinner that night, she had set a large brown paper bag on the table near my Circolectric bed. After she told me that she never doubted I would get better, she picked up the bag. She pulled out the penny loafers I had worn to school on the day of the accident.

I had never seen them so shiny.

CHAPTER 5

I had never thought of Randi as particularly brave, but she never once betrayed fear or loathing or pity when in my hospital room. Indeed, no visitor had ever cracked in my presence, except my father's Aunt Gert, whom I'd met only a few times before the accident. Eighty-year-old Gert, her puffy white cheeks rouged, her thinning bluish hair coiffed, entered one Saturday with handkerchief at the ready and was crying by the time she reached my bed. My mother escorted her out so quickly that I couldn't understand anything Gert said between sobs.

As soon as Gert left, her sister, my Grandma Fiffer, entered. Grandma was smaller and younger than Gert, although not as young as she claimed to be. "I'm thirty-nine," she'd say whenever we asked. And she dyed her hair brown to maintain the illusion. I would have expected her to fall apart, too. She still thought of me as a baby; on the Thanksgiving before I was hurt, she had brought me the Classic Comics version of *Moby Dick*.

On this, her first visit to the hospital, she approached tentatively. She stood by my bed, her upper lip quivering. "Here, sugar," she said. And she tried to hand me a one-dollar bill.

I couldn't hold it, much less spend it. Jim understood the absurdity of the situation. "Here, Grandma," he said gently. "I'll take that."

It was one thing that I had made a vow never to lose my composure or to worry in front of them. It was quite another thing that, except for Aunt Gert, my visitors universally survived the spectacle of me without flinching. I began to suspect a grand plot. I envisioned a corner of the hospital Solarium set aside for "Fiffer Briefings," where prospective visitors gathered like World War II pilots before an important flight. Standing before a diagram of the target—me—my mother, or perhaps Supreme Commander Meyer, explained the mission and cautioned, "Above all, stay cool."

And they did stay cool. No crying. No fainting. No stifled "OhmyGods." *What happens after they leave?* I wondered. *Do they offer my parents their condolences? Do they blow lunch?*

By the time I wiggled my toe, my sense of hearing had become immensely powerful, allowing me to see through closed doors, down distant corridors to know who was coming to visit. Footsteps were like fingerprints. Already I had scores on file.

"That's Mr. Martin coming," I predicted to Bill one afternoon as we watched Lew Alcindor and his UCLA teammates annihilate another opponent.

"How can you be so sure?" he asked.

I'd remind him that our former teacher weighed three hundred pounds and made quite a bit of noise as he clomped down the hall in his snow boots. "Besides, it's Sunday."

Mr. Martin, a bachelor in his mid-forties, came every Sunday after lunch and stayed for a few hours. This was very sweet. But Sunday was also the day my parents liked to bring Tommy, and between my large bed and the equally large Mr. M., there was little room for either a toddler or family small talk. Mr. Martin seemed oblivious to this, and no one had the heart to suggest he might be overstaying his welcome, particularly after he presented the hospital with a proposal to produce *Peter Pan* in the Solarium for me and my fellow patients. (The hospital, which did not want thirty sixth-graders delivering a variety of germs or illnesses in addition to their lines, politely demurred.)

Tommy usually managed to squeeze in. This may not have been for the best. Shortly after returning home from one visit, my mother grabbed him just before he threw himself down the long stairway leading from our second floor to the first floor. "What were you doing?" she screamed.

"I want a broken neck like Steve's," he said.

The footsteps of my yearbook adviser Mr. Frey were also distinctive. Mr. Frey moved at a quicker pace than Mr. Martin, but always paused outside the door, as if gathering the courage to enter. I understood why.

He had visited for the first time in mid-January, a couple of weeks after I wiggled my toe. By this time, things were looking up. Having hibernated for much of the winter, my toes and fingers on my left side were finally waking up. (They were still a bit groggy, however, and moved slowly and erratically.)

As Mr. Frey and I were discussing the strange case of my missing lunch—no one had ever found the brown bag I had left in the yearbook office on the day of the accident—I felt a tingle in my scalp. I have never been in an earthquake, but I imagine that what I experienced was similar to the first moments of such a phenomenon. The tingle was quickly followed by a rumble and then just as quickly by a violent shake as my tongs burst forth from my skull pulling the attached weights forward from behind the bed. Mr. Frey turned ghostly white. Frightened that any movement might upset the fusion, I sat as still as if I were totally paralyzed. "Please get a nurse," I whispered between clenched teeth.

One nurse summoned Dr. Meyer, while one nurse held my head immobile, and a third ministered to my shaken teacher. When the doctor arrived, he was unmiffed. "Well, these tongs are telling us they're about ready to come out," he said.

"I hope the catheter doesn't tell us the same way," I muttered.

The doctor removed the tongs for good a few days later, and my urologist Dr. Levine removed the catheter a few days after that to see if I could pee on my own. I could—although I only had about fifteen seconds between the time I felt the urge and the time I had to go. A urinal replaced the Foley bag at my side.

A few hours after the catheter was removed, Dr. Meyer came to my room bearing a life-sized plastic skull and spine. He hadn't been in the hospital the night that I wiggled my toe for everyone. When I had given him a command performance the next morning, he had apologized for doubting me. "I am going to get better, aren't I?" I had asked. "This proves it, doesn't it?" He had nodded affirmatively as he always did.

"Alas poor Yorick," I said motioning to the skull. Hamlet was still fresh in my mind from English class.

Meyer then explained my injury and how the spinal cord works. Then he told me that all of the doctors, himself included, had thought I'd never move again—at least below the waist. The return of the left toe and ankle was important, he continued, and so, too, was the return of urinary function. "You're a very pleasant miracle," he concluded. "And I for one have never been happier to have been proven wrong."

This was the first time anyone had told me that the doctors had been pessimistic. I thought back on all the times I had asked if I were going to be okay and my parents had said "Of course." They hadn't been totally honest.

I started to cry. I wasn't mad at them. I was glad they had lied. Something told me that if I had known from the beginning that I wasn't supposed to have started moving, I might not have started moving.

As the tears continued, I realized I wasn't only crying for myself, but for my parents. It must have been terrible getting the phone call from school, driving to the hospital, seeing me with two holes drilled into my head, watching me unable to move. And how much more terrible it must have been to hear that I would remain that way forever, and then, on top of that, to have to reassure me that everything was going to be all right.

Dr. Meyer left me alone with my thoughts. It was only later that I realized I hadn't asked him exactly when I was going to get back to normal.

.   .   .

I wasn't back to normal as February began and I entered my third month in the hospital. My left hand was functional enough so that I could now grab a pencil and follow along with Mr. Prince and my classmates. My left leg was strong enough so that I could squeeze it to my still motionless right leg—a feat I performed with regularity when Miss Boland, my favorite nurse from the floor, a young redhead only a few years older than I, was washing my crotch. "Sorry, spasm," I would lie. Then I'd count silently to ten before releasing her imprisoned hand from my balls.

I had just finished playing this game one Saturday when I heard an unfamiliar set of feet heading toward my door. "This must be the guy from Harvard," I said.

Both Harvard and Yale sent volunteer alums to interview applicants. The interviewer from Yale had visited me a few days earlier. To my surprise, I recognized him as William Jones. While in college, he had worked summers and winter breaks at Ray's Sports Shop in Glencoe. I remembered buying hockey equipment from him. To my even greater surprise, he recognized me. Although the tongs were out of my skull, from what I could tell by looking in a small mirror, I didn't look too much like myself. My skin was pale, my face was drawn, and my hair was flat and greasy.

The interview had gone well, I thought. Jones seemed comfortable at my bedside, and he appeared genuinely interested in persuading me that Yale was the right place for me, a better choice than Harvard or Stanford.

Those were my only possibilities. Because we had about nine hundred students in our senior class, New Trier would only process three applications per individual. The high school guidance counselors recommended applying to two colleges you really liked and one "safety" school—an institution that was certain to accept you. In addition to touring eastern campuses in October, I had visited Stanford with two classmates who were being recruited for the gymnastics team. The college had rolled out the red carpet for my friends, and Stanford's parallel bars specialist had hosted a fairly wild party in their honor. The late fall weather had been balmy and the campus clean and beautiful. The coeds were tan and pretty. And, oh yes, the classes we attended were interesting. I knew I wanted to apply there.

I had liked Harvard just as well. Dad and I had toured the campus with one of my friends from the New Trier Class of '67. Then we had watched him play in a freshman football game. The school seemed steeped in history. My friend was enthusiastic about his courses and social life. And I loved Boston. Two down, one to go.

Amherst was my third choice after I returned from the East. The campus was idyllic. The bright, beautiful, blond girls of Smith College were nearby. The core-curriculum concept appealed to me. And, oh yes, the director of admissions told me he thought I was a very strong candidate.

Yale trailed Amherst. I had liked the campus and the classes I had attended, but New Haven didn't measure up to Boston, Palo Alto, or western Massachusetts. In addition, my guide, a neighbor from Glencoe, was less enthusiastic about his school than his counterparts—although, to be honest, I'd never seen him enthusiastic about anything.

I begged the counselors to let me apply to four colleges. "The more schools, the better chance I've got of getting in," I argued.

A rule is a rule, they told me. They suggested that I forget about Amherst and Yale and apply to the University of Chicago as my safety school. They said that since I was the son of an active alumnus—my father helped with fundraising for the school—I stood an excellent chance of getting in.

"Never," I said. I didn't want to go to a school that my father had gone to; I wanted to get out from under his massive shadow and into college on my own. And I certainly didn't want to go to college an hour away from home. I was ready to live somewhere else, experience the East or West coast.

In the end, I decided to apply to Yale instead of Amherst because of a headline in the *Sun-Times*. The headline had nothing to do with the awarding of Nobel prizes or Rhodes scholarships. It wasn't about some remarkable discovery by a faculty member. Rather, it read in bold 18-point type: YALE BEATS HARVARD 24–20. A lengthy article followed. At the bottom of the page was a round-up of other eastern football scores. In minuscule 6-point agate type, the paper reported Williams 14, Amherst 10.

The decision suddenly seemed simple. Yale was as easy to differentiate from Amherst as 18-point bold type from 6-point agate. *You only get one shot at this. You're going big time,* I said to myself.

Though the loser in the football game, Harvard remained my first choice, and as the interviewer approached, I raised the bed to a proper angle, ran a comb through my hair, and hid the urinal. I need not have wasted the time. The alum, a beefy, red-faced man of about thirty, took one look at me, cleared his throat, and said, "Mmm, we can do this later if you like."

"No, it's fine. We can do it now," I said.

He didn't take his coat off during the entire five minutes he stayed. In between squirms, he did, however, look at his watch three times. Finally, he said that he had to be going.

"The alumni interview doesn't count very much anyway," said Rensy, who was applying to Harvard, Amherst, and Princeton, where his older brother was a junior. But just to get my goose, he added that he had been interviewed by the same Harvard alum later that same day and, "It went great. The guy seemed as if he wanted to stay all afternoon."

This was the old Rensy, not the docile shadow who had come that first night. It had taken him a while to regain his form. He had visited only sporadically during the first few weeks when I wasn't moving. And he had never come alone; his mother or his girlfriend, Sally, always accompanied him. Once, he and Sally had entered just as two of my other friends were leaving. "That's the guy who broke Steve's neck," I heard one say to the other in the hallway. I assume Rensy heard it, too. He had stayed away for a week after that. But now, with me on the mend, he came by himself almost daily. (He had the visitor's passes, which he impishly collected instead of turning back in, to prove this.) I could almost chart my progress by the frequency of his gibes and his visits.

My mother was in the room as we discussed the interviews. Now my father entered. "The specialist from Michael Reese Hospital is here," he said.

Rensy exited as a tiny man who looked to be in his early sixties entered the room with authority. He wore a thin black bow tie and a charcoal gray suit. He carried an umbrella and a black doctor's bag. Save a black pencil mustache and black pencil eyebrows, time had erased all of his hair. His lips had retreated into his mouth.

"I am Dr. Graham," the man announced.

Mom, who was standing closest to the door, smiled and offered her hand. Graham handed her his umbrella. I didn't like him. I didn't care that he was touted as the best "physiatrist" (whatever that was) in Chicago. There was no need for someone to come in and tell us about the future. I was going to walk out of the hospital just as soon as my right leg started working.

In a deep and powerful voice that almost made me forget

how small and rude he was, Dr. Graham told me that his time was limited and that he planned to administer several tests. After insisting on complete silence, he opened his bag. He gave Nurse Masters a printed sheet and instructed her to fill in the appropriate blanks with the numbers he would be calling out. I was to move various parts of my body on command.

"Big left toe," said Graham. I wiggled. "Three," the doctor told Masters.

"What's the highest?" I asked.

No response.

"Ankle."

Not quite as strong.

"Two."

"That came back after the toes," I offered.

"No need for commentary, young man."

After a series of scores—left wrist 3; left quadriceps 2; right ankle 0—I said, "Bingo!"

Graham did not smile. He took a tuning fork out of the bag, told me to shut my eyes, and applied the fork to my left ankle. "What's that?" he asked.

"F-sharp?" I giggled.

Mom laughed. The doctor threatened to stop the test.

Several touches later, Graham put the tuning fork away and pulled a pin and a feather from his bag. I was to tell him whether I was being pricked or tickled. In most cases I could distinguish the difference—thank goodness. When I couldn't, I opened my eyes and cheated.

Cheating was more difficult when he asked if he was touching me with a hot test tube or a cold one. They looked exactly alike. When in doubt, I guessed cold; it seemed much better suited to his temperament.

Finally finished, Graham gave me a condescending nod and motioned for my mother and father to go outside with him. Because my hearing was a "ten," I could pick up their conversation down the hallway. "Your son is extremely fortunate to be moving at all," Graham said. "I would opine that his left leg will experience a moderate—"

I started whistling. I didn't want to hear this.

Some of Graham's words filtered through my whistle. "Prognosis." "Therapy." I whistled more loudly. "Stand." "Wheelchair." "Productive." I hummed. That was better, but I still got the gist of what he was saying: I was never going to get out of a wheelchair (I hadn't even been out of the bed and into a wheelchair yet). My left leg might possibly be strong enough to support me some day, but my right leg—which still wasn't working at all—would probably never work. And even if it did, it would always be too weak. And even if by some miracle I was able to stand, my hands would never be strong enough to grip the crutches I'd need to walk.

George Matthews, the man who had been in the Intensive Care Unit with me broke almost every bone in his body except his neck. He is now in the private room next door to mine. Earlier this week, the doctors removed his last cast. He now maneuvers on two canes. I feel happy for George. But I also feel jealous. No, *angry*. He's sixty years old. He's had a full life. Why is he walking, while I'm not? What the hell have I done in my seventeen years to deserve this? How could I have made God so mad?

When I was younger, I used to sneak a radio into temple during the High Holidays so I could listen to the World Series. And this last Yom Kippur, I caused a big stink at home by saying I wasn't going to wear a tie to services, that I could be even more religious if I weren't being choked at the neck. But surely even if these are sins, they don't deserve the punishment I've received.

Sometimes I've been a cocky smartass. Okay, most of the time I've been a cocky smartass. But again, couldn't God have put me in my place some other way—maybe by having me turned down at all the colleges I'm applying to?

There's one explanation that's so scary I try not to think about it. At Northwestern's Cherubs, I told Luskin about a girl from New York I had met in Florida the previous summer. I remembered that I was about six months late in responding to her last letter. "Let's think of a good excuse," I said. Together we composed a letter explaining that I hadn't written because I had been paralyzed in a car accident. We sent it off five months before I really was hurt.

Could this be my punishment for that? Does God really work that way?

Our superstitious cleaning lady Willie Bee has offered a different theory. "The Lord only tests those He thinks are strong enough to survive," she told me the last time she visited.

I think she's right. This is my test.

So screw Dr. Graham. Screw all the other doctors who had thought—might still think—I'll never walk again.

I am doing all I can to get better. Trying my hardest with Mr. Cole when he gives me physical therapy. Doing the exercises he has given me to do on my own. Staying in a positive frame of mind so the body's own healing powers can be brought to bear. Drinking a glass of water every hour so that I won't get a bladder infection. Eating the right foods to restore my strength. Taking my medicine. Getting my rest. Saying my prayers.

I have never tolerated losing and I am not going to lose my future. I am going to beat this. I am going to walk out of the hospital. Wind up with Randi or some other beauty in my arms just the way James Bond does. I am going to Harvard in the fall.

My life has been easy. By the luck of the draw, I've been graced with intelligent, stable, supportive parents; born into financial comfort; grown up in a healthy, functional household; been encouraged to be the best; been told that I was the best.

It's time I face a challenge. My father has overcome challenges throughout his life. My mother has raised me to be a leader. It is time to prove I am a man. I didn't ask for this particular test, but it was almost inevitable, wasn't it? We Fiffers don't do things small.

CHAPTER 6

"Bath time," said Mr. Weston, my male nurse. The pale, chunky, forty-year-old with a receding blond hairline set the pink plastic wash basin by the Circolectric bed. "Let me empty that urinal first," he said.

Weston had replaced Masters about three weeks earlier. A few days after Dr. Graham's visit, Dr. Meyer had decided that it was time for me to start sitting in a wheelchair. Masters had departed because transferring me from bed to chair was akin to moving heavy cargo from a ship's deck to a dock and required the strength of a longshoreman.

Weston had never worked the waterfront, but he was much better equipped than the diminutive Masters to move a 170-pound load of flab. The procedure required timing and balance as well as muscle. First, a sling attached to an automated hoist was placed under my butt. Then the hoist was activated and I rose slowly into the airspace above the mattress. At this critical point, as I swayed to and fro, the nurse had to grab the sides of the sling and swing me over the side of the bed to a point directly above the chair. This done, the hoist was reactivated and I was lowered into the seat.

I had been terrified the first few times that we had tried this.

What if something went wrong, and I fell and broke my neck again? I was about as powerless to help as a crate full of bananas, but I soon came to trust Weston, who had huge hands and a (justifiably) huge ego when it came to his strength and his nursing skills. I was glad a man was in charge now—except for the bathing part.

Once in the chair, I could actually leave my room. Weston would push me to the Solarium, where for the first several days I was content just to look out the big window and see trees and snow and cars and people. I saw people in the Solarium, too, and television on a set that was ever so much bigger than the little one over my bed. And, it was in color.

It was mid-March. I had been in the hospital for more than three months. My world was getting bigger again. But Dr. Meyer refused to offer a timetable whenever I asked when I might go home. "You're doing better," he'd say. "But you'll have to be stronger. Let's just see."

I was doing better. I could now raise my left leg an inch or so off the bed and bend my knee slightly. I still couldn't wiggle my right toes, but I was able to move the right leg from side to side just a little and could consciously tighten my calf muscle.

This pattern of gradual recovery was almost as mystifying as it was gratifying. The left side had been reborn in the toes and was working its way up. Why was the right side starting at the top and working its way down? The doctors said they didn't know.

I began to think of my two legs as if they were my two brothers. My left leg was like Jim. It required attention from time to time to help it flourish, but it was fairly self-sufficient. I wouldn't dare forget about it, but I could concentrate my efforts on the needier right leg. This leg, like little Tommy, couldn't be expected to function if left on its own. It required constant diligence, and I devoted myself to its welfare. Unfortunately, at the moment, righty was as obstinate and temperamental as a two-year-old child, refusing to do what I told it and offering no explanation for its intransigence. *Just a phase,* I told myself.

Weston returned from emptying the urinal. He pulled my bedsheet down to my ankles, and I quickly floated to the ceiling. I watched as he picked the lint from my penis and then lathered my balls with soap. His face was impassive; he could have been picking lint from a sweater, lathering his own chin for a shave. My face said, *Let's get this over with.* There would be no phony spasms to trap his hand down there.

"Big day, huh?" he said.

Just finish the goddamn bath, then we'll talk, I thought. But I said, "Yep."

"Nervous?" he asked.

"Nervous about what?" my mother asked as she came in the door.

I pulled the sheet up over my waist with my left hand. "Do you mind?" I said. I wasn't sure what was worse: getting bathed by Weston or having my mother in the room while I was being bathed.

"Sorry," Mom said. "Here, Mr. Weston." She handed him a pair of gray dress pants and a blue turtleneck. "This is what you asked for," she said to me. "Your dad's in the Solarium. I'll go wait with him."

"Next time knock," I said as she left.

"A little testy, aren't we?" asked Weston.

He towels me off and begins to dress me. For the first time in over a hundred days, I am going to wear clothes. For the first time in over a hundred days, I am going to put on the shoes that Mom polished that first night. For the first time in over a hundred days, I'm going to leave the hospital, albeit only for a few hours to attend a debate banquet at the high school.

The first thing to go on is a device that hardly qualifies as clothing. Weston straps a foot-long rubber bag to my left leg. The bag is designed to hold urine. I've regained more control of my bladder, but when the urge to pee comes, I still can't turn it off like everybody else can. Thus, Dr. Levine, the urologist, has provided the leg bag for our field trip.

Tubing extends from each end of the bag. The bottom tube, only three or four inches in length, is clamped at its end. The top tube extends from knee to thigh up to the penis, where it is connected to another tube. This last tube is itself attached to a condom which Weston secures with a special adhesive spray. Dr. Levine has assured me that the system is 95 percent leakproof. While this is comforting, I still feel the hookup chokes my manhood. I was hoping to wear a condom this year, but not for this.

A second piece of equipment is wrapped around my waist— an elastic white corset, perhaps five inches wide. I got woozy the first time I sat up. Held together with Velcro, the new fastening material that sticks to itself, the corset is designed to improve my circulation.

The real clothes leave no doubt that my body is still on vacation. The turtleneck hangs loosely over my atrophied upper body; the pants are about three inches too small in the waist. I look like a starving child of Africa—caved-in chest, bloated belly. Weston pulls the shirt down and leaves the slacks unbuttoned. The shoes—purely ceremonial today as I cannot stand, much less walk—feel funny. My feet, bare all these weeks, quickly become claustrophobic.

The final piece: a stainless steel neck brace with a padded chin support connected to two parallel bars extending to a mid-chest plate. I don't think I have to worry about someone else wearing the same outfit to this evening's affair. Weston locks me in.

Leg bag, corset, neck brace. I am a knight armored for battle. But the enemy is neither a rival knight nor a vicious dragon, but my own uncontrollable body.

In a perfect world, I would be going to a gathering of yearbook or soccer friends or getting together with Bill and our card partners Larry and Nemo for an evening of hearts instead of meeting fellow debate team members with whom I'm not particularly close. Then again, in a perfect world, I wouldn't be strapped into a wheelchair unable to walk.

The team has been kind enough to send a yellow van. Unfortunately, Weston can't fit the chair in upright. I ride the entire twenty minutes tipped back at a sixty-degree angle, wondering with each bump if the fusion will withstand the shock. Because of the position of my chair, everything is cockeyed, tilted. Trees look as if their branches are connected to the ground, store signs as if they are written in a foreign language

We finally arrive. As Weston wheels me in, I begin to feel dizzy. I move my left hand first to the leg bag to make sure it is secure and then to my right hand to make sure it looks like the hand it is supposed to be instead of the claw it has become. With help, the right fingers open up briefly, but then curl back up like an anemone that has been disturbed by an unwelcome intruder.

The dizziness intensifies. My eyes and mind are getting

blurry. Is the corset letting me down? Or is this a different kind of circulation problem? Is it possible that I'm afraid to be circulating among classmates who aren't among my closest friends, in the building where I was hurt?

As we approach the lunch hall where the banquet is being held, I suddenly imagine that a surprise party in my honor is waiting behind the doors. Balloons and posters welcoming my return, the marching band set to play "For He's a Jolly Good Fellow," cheering pompon girls forming an aisle leading to a makeshift stage where the principal stands ready to deliver a speech full of superlatives and a plaque recognizing my courage, newspaper and television reporters to capture the moment for posterity.

I rally. I take a deep breath and prepare to act surprised. And I am surprised, truly. For my return is apparently no big deal.

The lunch hall looks just as it did in December. The only posters on the tall lime green walls extol the virtues of Student Council candidates. No band. No balloons. No pompon girls or principal. The most distinguished school official is our debate coach, Mr. Boyd. I realize I have become too accustomed to being the center of attention.

Some debaters do move toward me. The handful who have visited me in the hospital appear much more comfortable than those who haven't. The no-shows approach more cautiously, either uneasy with my appearance or guilty for not visiting. I feel the stares of the freshmen and sophomores, pink-skinned and nameless, who have joined the team since I was hurt and know little about me.

I am in the real world. For the first time in four months, I am with people who have not made a conscious decision that they want to be with me. For a moment, I'm struck with the eerie feeling that I feel more comfortable in my hospital room. I should never have come here.

Roger Scully, my debate partner, hangs back until I'm alone again. He hasn't changed in the last hundred days—still short and thin, still sporting a crewcut, still wearing white socks with dark pants and a sportcoat. Sometimes my family will play a game where we list the names of those who have surprised us by coming through since the accident—friends whom we didn't realize were so loyal or strong or close. We also list those who have disappointed us—those who apparently don't like us as much as we thought or are too weak to deliver. Roger stands close to the top of this second list. He has never come to the hospital or even called.

"Hey, Steve," Roger says. If this were a debate tournament, I'd mark him down for failure to make eye contact.

"Hey, Roger."

"How's it going?" he asks.

I know I should take the high road here. Instead, I say this: "I could be better. The big problem right now are these stitches the doctors put in. They really itch." I scratch my stomach. Roger shifts uneasily from one foot to the other. I'd give him low marks for posture, too. "Actually," I continue, "I'm thinking about pulling them out. This is the first time I've been away from the hospital, so I might do it tonight. Here." I reach under my turtleneck.

Roger pulls back. "Your doctors must know what they're doing. I wouldn't pull them out."

I scratch again. "I just can't take it anymore." I find the Velcro fastener on the corset and begin to pull. Rrrripp. It certainly sounds painful. I wince.

Roger winces. "Don't, Steve."

I pull again. Rrrripp. I gasp.

"I, uh, think it's time for dinner," Roger says. "I'll catch you later."

Have a nice life, Rog.

Dinnertime. Weston wheels me to a table where three of my closer friends on the team sit. "I'm going to grab a cigarette," he says. "I'll be back in fifteen."

The dining hall crew, working overtime, serves us our food—London broil, baked potatoes, and canned green beans. I hadn't even thought about the logistics of eating tonight. What am I going to do? I can handle a fork, but not a knife. In the hospital, Mom or Dad or Weston cuts my food for me. How long until Weston comes back? I know I can spear the beans, but the foil-wrapped potato and the meat have a much better chance of ending up in my lap than my mouth.

"Something wrong?" asks the server.

Even if Weston were here, I wouldn't let him cut my food in front of all these people.

"I forgot this was for dinner," I lie. "I already ate."

I do drink a glass of water. No sooner have I finished than I feel the urge to pee. I make sure my dinner companions aren't looking, then reach down to feel if the condom and tubing are properly in place (although there wouldn't be time to do anything if they weren't). Everything seems in order, and I feel the not unpleasant warmth of my urine as it moves through the tube to my leg bag.

Dodged that bullet. If it had leaked, I would have "accidentally" spilled my drinking water on my pants to create a decoy stain. And these gray pants would stain. I make a mental note to wear something darker next time.

Now I move my hand down to the bag itself. It's full. Where is Weston? We should empty this before I have to go again.

"Ready to hit the little boy's room?" Weston says when he returns a few minutes later.

Is the bag's bulge that noticeable?

The bathroom is empty, thank God. Weston wheels me to the stall. "Damn," he says. The chair is too wide for the door.

"Now what?" I want to be done with this before anyone else comes in.

Weston enters the stall, then pulls my chair as close to the opening as possible. "Lift your leg," he says.

Why don't we just go outside and find a fire hydrant?

I raise my left leg a few inches off the metal footrest. Weston then guides it to the edge of the toilet bowl. Once the leg is secure, he reaches into my sock and finds the short piece of tubing attached to the bottom of the leg bag. He takes off the small metal clamp and whoosh! the dam is open and the river of urine rushes into the john.

"Oh, excuse me." Roger Scully stands at the door.

"He pees into a bag just like the astronauts," Weston says.

"Please don't tell anyone, Roger."

I watch him the rest of the evening to see if he keeps his promise to guard my secret. Every time I see him start a conversation, every time I see him standing in a group, I cringe.

Why is this so important to me? I'm sitting in a wheelchair, locked in a neck brace, unable to stand on my own, unable to move half my body, and I'm worried that the world will learn that I'm peeing into plastic?

I know why. I'm afraid that the girls I know will think I'm less manly. Less manly for what? It's not like I could jump out of this chair and sweep them into bed if I didn't have the bag.

It's not as if I had ever swept any of them into bed before I got hurt.

Back at the hospital, we wheel past a young man who is limping. "Would you settle for that?" Weston asks.

"No way."

I just know everything is going to be all right.

After Weston goes home and I'm alone in my room, I call upon God as I do each night. I understand what *quid pro quo* means because I have taken three years of Latin, and because I've watched my father in action. "Okay, what do you want?" I ask out loud. "I'll lie in a tub of shit for six months if I can walk away from this. I'll pee in my pants in front of Randi Miller. I'll let them cut off a finger or two, if you'll make my right leg work."

I assume my parents are trying to cut their own deals with the Almighty for my recovery, so sometimes I include them in my negotiations—never without their permission, however. "Mom," I asked one day, "would you cut off your little finger if it meant I could walk?"

She nodded.

"What about *two* fingers?"

"Why don't you do the exercises," she said.

"For your information, I'm doing my butt squeezes as we speak," I said.

I had asked Mr. Cole for a routine I could do on my own. One exercise involved squeezing my buttocks together ten times. Another involved tightening my leg muscles and pushing down into the mattress. The therapist also instructed me to try and arch my back and lift my hips off the bed.

The extra exercising was paying off. A few days after my trip to the high school, Dr. Meyer said he thought I was ready to stand. Not on the floor, but in, or rather on, the Circolectric bed. Instead of strapping me to the board and turning the bed the full 180 degrees until I was facing the floor, Weston was to stop when I was upright, at 90 degrees.

On our first effort, the room got fuzzy after about ten seconds and I quickly signaled for Weston to bring me back down before I passed out. Dr. Meyer explained that my blood was pooling in my feet and seemed in no hurry to return to my brain. "Let's tighten the corset and start at forty-five degrees and work our way up," he said.

Jim said that strapped to the moving bed, trying to tolerate gravity, I reminded him of an astronaut. The way my ears were ringing, I thought of myself more like Odysseus, lashed to the mast of his ship, trying to avoid the songs of the Sirens.

Within a week or so I could tolerate a couple of minutes at ninety degrees. This, coupled with a noticeable increase in the strength of my right leg, led Dr. Meyer to conclude I was ready to try standing on terra firma. Early in April, Weston wheeled me to the hospital's Physical Therapy Department for the first time. There, he and Mr. Cole locked me into a pair of metal braces that extended from ankle to hip. The therapist positioned the chair at the entrance to a set of parallel bars, and then he and Weston lifted me up as if I were the Tin Woodsman in *The Wizard of Oz*. I held on to the bars for dear life with my functional left hand and almost totally useless right one. The men stood at my side, their arms strategically placed on my back and stomach to prevent me from caving in. The braces forbade me from bending my legs, so I just stood there, suppressing the urge to giggle, trying not to show my excitement at having reached this new milestone. I lasted about a minute before tiring. They lowered me back into the chair, I rested, and then I tried again.

I would have stayed all afternoon, but after a few more attempts, Mr. Cole made me go back to my room. "You're gonna hurt like heck tomorrow morning," he said. I did—and I loved the feeling. This was the kind of pain that I used to feel after a long soccer practice or a two-mile portage or a handball match. I wanted more.

The news that I was standing in the parallel bars excited most everyone in the hospital who had been following my case for the last four months. I had become good friends with Dr. Levine, a transplanted New Yorker who looked and sounded like Woody Allen and had a sense of humor to match. He proposed that we celebrate by taking a field trip to see comedian Don Rickles, who was performing at a club in Chicago. Weston came along to transfer me in and out of the doctor's car. Randi joined us, too. I actually had a date!

The morning after this big night out, Miss Lennard asked me to stay on the line after Latin because someone had some important news for me. One of her students then proceeded to tell me that I had been accepted at Harvard. April 15 was the day we were supposed to hear from colleges; that was almost two weeks away. Was this a joke? No, said the student. His father headed the Harvard Alumni Club in Chicago and had received an advance list.

I phoned my father at the office right away. He was suspicious of my calls—for good reason. Half the time I phoned just to pull his leg. A few weeks earlier, I had breathlessly proclaimed that I had completed the impossible Double-Crostic puzzle at the back of the *Saturday Review*. Dad proudly relayed word of this achievement to a client sitting across from him before realizing that I had struck again.

The Harvard story seemed less believable than the Double-Crostic one. I finally convinced him that I had indeed received the good news. "Let's just keep this quiet until the letter comes," he said. I reluctantly agreed to keep the news within the family.

It was a good thing, too. When my three letters arrived on April 15, two were thick and one was thin. I had been accepted at Stanford and Yale, but rejected by Harvard. I was sure there had been some mistake. My father made a couple of calls and was told that Harvard had determined I would not be physically capable of attending.

How stupid could they be? I was standing in parallel bars. It was only a matter of time before I started walking again.

"Screw Harvard," I told my friends. "If they don't want me, I don't want them." I would be delighted to prove the school wrong just as I had proved Meyer and Graham wrong, and all the others who had doubted me.

Two days later I took my first step in the bars. And the day after that I doubled my output. "It's time for you to go home," said Dr. Meyer.

PART TWO

Prior to discharge, the patient had been walking (in parallel bars) with the help of people holding onto him, (but) had poor control of the right lower extremity. His main problem at the time of discharge was the persistent triceps weakness in both arms and weakness of the right lower extremity. . . . The pt. had full range of motion of his neck, solid fusion by X-ray of C4 through C6. There was weakness of the trunk muscles. He had good function of the left hand, fair function with the right hand. He had very poor finger control on the right. . . . He had very little function below the right knee. He was barely able to move the toes on the right foot. Pt. was to have physical therapy on discharge and continue with muscle strengthening and walking.

Highland Park Hospital discharge record, 4/26/68

CHAPTER 7

I was still in bed, waiting for Weston, when the phone rang. A few minutes later, my mother came into the first-floor study that had been serving as my bedroom during the three weeks I had been home from the hospital. Still in a wheelchair, still extremely weak in the trunk and on my right side, I could not manage the fourteen stairs leading to the second floor and the door marked STEVO.

My mother yawned, then scratched the sleep from her eyes. Once awake and infused with the first of her daily dozen cups of coffee, she was impossible to keep up with. But she had not been an early riser since Jim and I were in elementary school. Our constant teasing at breakfast—more properly, *my* constant teasing—drove her back to her bedroom, where I suspect she waited until she heard us close the door and then sprang up for that first Camel (nonfilter) and shot of Maxwell House (black). She had somehow managed to train Tommy to sleep until the coast was clear. She had been getting up earlier since I'd been home from the hospital after four months, two weeks, and six days—not that I was counting—but not this early.

"Your nurse just phoned," Mom said. "His daughter is running a fever. He won't be in."

Dad had long since left for work. Jim was already off to school. Mom's eyes were so bad that she drove only on the North Shore, where she knew the streets and other markers. She couldn't get me to where I had to go downtown. "How am I gonna get out of bed and get to the Rehab?" I demanded.

For the last two weeks, Weston had been dressing me, loading me into the wheelchair, and driving me down to the Rehabilitation Institute of Chicago (RIC), where I received physical therapy. Dr. Meyer had suggested I transfer directly from the hospital to the RIC as an inpatient. My parents had agreed that this was the wisest move from a logistical standpoint, but had nevertheless decided I should commute from home as an outpatient. "If he lives there, he might start to feel he belongs there," I heard Dad tell Dr. Meyer outside my hospital room one evening shortly before I was discharged. "I don't want him to think he's part of that world." He went on to say that if I were home, doing things with family and friends who weren't in wheelchairs and worse, I'd think of myself as normal and progress faster.

I had initially wanted to continue therapy at Highland Park as an outpatient. "I feel comfortable here," I had told Dad. I didn't want to go to a place where they didn't know me. I also thought it might jinx my progress if I went somewhere else.

"This is nonnegotiable," said Dad, who had researched rehab centers across the country and had already pulled strings to circumvent the institute's three-month waiting list. "RIC is one of the top three places in the U.S., and you're going there."

On my first day there, I realized that once again my parents had made the right decision. The institute, housed a few blocks northeast of the Loop in what had been a six-story warehouse, was geared toward helping someone with my kind of injury. The therapists were more experienced and the equipment was better. Moreover, the man overseeing my therapy, Dr. Betts, immediately understood what was driving me—my desire to go off to college in September. On time. Like everyone else.

I had decided to go to Yale instead of Stanford for three reasons. First, based on my campus visits, I was convinced that Yale would make me buckle down academically more than Stanford would. I had been too casual a student in high school; I knew I needed an environment where I would work harder. Second, Dr. Keggi, who had performed the anterior fusion, was in New Haven; I felt safer knowing that he would be nearby if I needed him. And finally, I felt more secure knowing that many friends would be at nearby schools. Bill was going to Denver, but my friend Larry was heading for Penn, and Rensy had been accepted at Princeton.

Dr. Betts had also gone to Princeton. Although he teased me about my decision to go to "a second-rate college," he clearly considered me a kindred spirit. Few patients at the institute had their eyes set on the Ivy League. Whether fair or unfair, the fact that I seemed to have a good future ahead of me moved most of my caregivers there to give me special treatment, as did the fact that I had already recovered more than anyone had expected and also seemed to have good prospects for even more recovery.

As RIC's director, Dr. Betts, a tall, sandy-haired, elegant, impeccably tailored man of about forty, spent much of his time charting the future course of the institution and raising funds.

Considered one of the best rehabilitation doctors in the country, he supervised the care of only a handful of patients. Dad had cashed in a favor from a mutual friend to enable me to become one of the doctor's chosen few.

I was glad my parents had decided I should be an outpatient at the institute. Although there were some evening trips for which the inpatients were loaded en masse onto special buses, it seemed to me that the nights there must be incredibly long—just as they had been when I was in the hospital. In the meantime, our house had quickly been transformed into a community teen center.

The transformation had begun the night after I got home, with a large barbeque for all my friends who had visited me at the hospital. After that, guys and girls dropped in almost every night—as our loaded refrigerator and the bills for ice cream and soda pop attested. We played cards, watched the Cubs or Sox on TV, or played a game we made up called "off the wall." From my wheelchair strategically positioned in the middle of the backyard, I tried to catch tennis balls that my friends or Jim threw against the second story brick wall that sat over the angled roof of our family room addition. If the throw came near my left hand, I was pretty good.

One important name was missing from the roster of friends playing off the wall and other games. After coming to the barbeque, Randi had never returned. Indeed, we had not spoken since that night. I had phoned every evening for more than a week, but her mother always answered the phone and said Randi was studying. "Please ask her to call," I pleaded. But she never did.

I was confused and devastated. I couldn't think of anything I had said or done to cause Randi to disappear. I felt we had been closer after I was hurt than when we were going out. When we had gone to see Don Rickles, I had felt more special with her by my side than I had when we walked the halls of New Trier. Her presence sent a message to the world and to me: if this pretty girl is willing to date me, I must be okay.

I asked myself all sorts of questions: Was she acting all that time during those soul-baring late-night calls? Was it her plan from day one to help get me from hospital to home and then bow out? Was she being friendly out of pity? Or did I look so bad now that I was out of the hospital that she couldn't stomach being around me? I didn't think I looked *that* bad when cleaned and dressed and transferred from the wheelchair to a chair in our family room.

Unfortunately, Weston accomplished all of those acts for me. Thus, on the morning my bleary-eyed mother told me that he had phoned to say he wasn't coming, I panicked. I could not get myself out of bed without him, and I couldn't afford to miss a day of therapy at the Rehab.

Mom surveys the scene. The rented hospital bed sits where the rolltop desk used to be; the wheelchair rests in the corner previously occupied by a reading chair. To the left of the bed, under the still life of a table with apples and flowers, is my table—*Still Life in Hospital Supplies*. On it rest urinal, bedpan, tubing. "I guess I should have paid more attention to the way Weston gets you up," she says. "Let me get a cup of coffee and then we'll do the best we can."

"Empty the urinal first," I instruct her when she returns. "Then refill the water pitcher. And don't mix them up."

"Very funny."

When Weston is here, the bath comes next. The thought of

being bathed by my mother at age seventeen makes me feel particularly helpless, not to mention uncomfortable. "Maybe I can do without it today," I offer.

"Don't be silly. What's the procedure?"

"Fill the pot with lukewarm water and bring a couple of washcloths."

She spills some water on the floor. "Jesus, you're a klutz," I say.

"Oh, shut up," she snaps back, handing me a wet washcloth.

"What's this for?"

"So you can wash yourself."

"Me? I don't do it. Weston does."

"Your whole body? Why? You can do your face and most of the upper part, can't you? I can understand why he helps. But why does he do it all?"

"Because that's the way we do it. It's faster that way."

"Well, I don't think that's a very good reason. But we're running late. We'll discuss this later."

"We'll discuss this later," I mock. Then: "You can skip the crotch."

She does. "Now what?" she asks.

"Teeth. Put some toothpaste on the brush there."

"You're not capable of doing that?"

"I suppose I am. But Weston does it."

"Why?"

I push up on my elbows for added height. "What is this, the Inquisition?"

She hands me the toothbrush. "Do you want me to brush them for you, too?"

"Very funny."

We struggle for five minutes with my shirt, a loose-fitting blue pullover which she can't manage to slip over my weak right arm. I blame this on her ineptitude, and she walks out twice, the second time when the shirt is locked over my face. I'm just about free when she returns carrying a shirt with buttons. It slips on easily.

"Okay, button it," she says.

"Me?"

"What is going on here, Steve? What has this whole struggle been for? Is it that you *can't* do anything for yourself or just *don't* do anything?"

I push the button to move the bed to its most upright position. "That's not fair. I go down to Rehab and bust my ass for six hours a day."

"Well, it seems to me you should be busting your ass for an extra half hour here as well."

We're both silent as she puts my socks and undershorts on me. My bladder remains weak, so I still wear the leg bag during the day. She picks it up. "This smells," she says.

"Jesus Christ. It's none of your business. Will you just hurry, please."

She tries to connect the condom to the tubing. I refuse to watch this or think about the next step, attaching the condom to me.

The condom and the tube refuse to meet. After several fruitless minutes, she gives up. "Couldn't you go without this today?"

"I'll piss in my pants if it's not on." I'm not kidding around. This has happened a few times.

"Well, I can't do this. I'm going to call Dr. Levine. Maybe he can explain it to me over the phone."

While she's dialing, Tommy comes in. Mom pushes him away. He starts crying.

Dr. Levine offers to come over, hook me up, and then drive me to the Rehab, which is on his way to his office in the city. When he arrives, Mom—fortified by more coffee and the first of her daily sixty Camels, launches into her editorial. "I had no idea that Steve was so dependent," she begins.

"I'm listening," says Levine.

"Well," Mom continues, "I guess we've all been so busy congratulating ourselves on this remarkable recovery that we've forgotten how much he still has to learn again."

My mother has always had a talent for speaking to me by speaking to others.

"Keep talking, Elaine," Levine says. Then to me, "Can you get Shorty down there to cooperate so I can hook up this *shmatke.*"

"My feeling is that Mr. Weston senses that the longer he keeps Steve helpless, the longer he'll be drawing a paycheck here. We should have kept a closer watch on things."

"May I say something?" I ask.

"No, schmuck," says the doctor. "Elaine, hand me the spray there and keep talking."

Dow, the same company that is making the world safe for democracy by supplying the napalm we use in Vietnam, is making me safe by supplying the adhesive that keeps the condom from pulling off.

"College starts in September. How's he going to go to Yale if he can't even bathe himself or get dressed on his own? All our friends say we're crazy to let him go that far away. Maybe we should try and get him into Northwestern."

"No way," I shout. I'm not going to a college fifteen min-

utes away from my front door, where my parents can monitor my every move. Going to Yale would prove I have beaten
the injury. Going to Northwestern would be a compromise.
And "compromise" isn't in my vocabulary.

"Independence" is in my vocabulary, but as my mother is
pointing out, talk is cheap. "Well, if you don't want to go to
Northwestern, you better learn to start doing things for yourself," she continues.

"I can't. If I could do everything for myself, I'd be walking,
too."

"I didn't say everything, but you can put toothpaste on a
toothbrush, and I'll bet you could figure out how to slip a shirt
on. When your father and I went to look at the Rehabilitation
Institute, they showed us a whole area where they taught people tips for daily living. If I were you, young man, I'd sign up
today."

"Maybe you're right if the alternative is listening to this
crap every morning for the rest of the summer."

"Voilà," Levine says, breaking the tension. The condom is
on. "Steven, you don't have to worry if a girl asks you if you're
carrying protection."

Levine drops me off at the elevator in the Rehab Institute
lobby. I'm embarrassed to tell him that I've never wheeled myself, that Weston does all the pushing. Instead, I say that I'll get
up to physical therapy on my own.

I put my hands on the wheels and begin pushing the chair
forward. My left hand does fine, but my weak right one keeps
getting stuck in the spokes. I try to move forward one-handed,
but I keep going in a circle. An orderly finally helps me onto
the elevator and then wheels me to physical therapy.

I wait for my therapist in a reception area full of patients:

an older woman in a wheelchair, one hand cradled in a sling, spit slowly crawling down her chin; a young black man with only one leg and a horribly scarred stump glaring from his shorts; a girl of perhaps ten, badly burned, her skin the texture of a well-cooked Thanksgiving turkey.

I nod but do not speak. Dad's plan to isolate me from the abnormal has worked. I have made no friends here. In fact, I have made a conscious effort to avoid any involvements with the patients. If an outsider who didn't know any better looked at those of us sitting here, he might not see that I am different from the others. But I am. Some of them are going to be affected forever by what has happened to them. They are permanent residents of their conditions. I'm just a visitor passing through.

On my first day here, I was shocked to see the variety of injuries and illnesses that had befallen people—broken necks and backs from car crashes, football collisions, diving accidents, and falls off ladders, roofs, horses; spinal cords torn apart by urban gunfire, North Vietnamese snipers, doctors' wayward scalpels; limbs lost to hungry farm machinery, electrocution, diabetes; paralysis from strokes, hemorrhages, too little oxygen at birth. People who are the victims of their own folly. People who are the victims of others. People like me with no one to blame. I see them all and wonder what the hell I am doing in such company.

Mrs. Walsh, my therapist, picks me up promptly at nine-thirty. She is a small woman in her early thirties, with curly brown hair, and a face so large and round that her small blue eyes and button nose look like afterthoughts.

The PT Department occupies an entire floor of the institute. In one corner are the white-sheeted mats and therapy tables.

Adjacent to these are a series of parallel bars and mirrors. Pulleys extend from one of the cream-colored walls, as do three captain's wheels with special handles. (I remember playing endlessly with Rensy on something similar in kindergarten—not, however, for the purpose of strengthening my arms.) Practice stairs sit in another corner along with chairs designed for leg exercises. In a separate room there is a wading tank. Walking is easier in water.

My first hour in PT is divided into two parts. For the first forty minutes, I lie on the table or a mat and Mrs. Walsh takes my body through a series of patterned exercises. In one, I start with my arm above my head, move it diagonally to my hip, and then bring it back up again. In another, I lift my left leg up, then bend it, and bring my knee up toward my chest. She offers resistance to the stronger muscles and helps those that are weaker or not working at all through the range of motion.

I spend the last twenty minutes at the parallel bars, simply walking back and forth holding onto the bar. Dr. Graham, the specialist, was wrong. I'm standing and walking in the bars with the help of a metal brace on my right leg that extends from my shoe to just under my knee. This keeps the joint from giving out and picks up the still-dormant right foot.

After PT, I move one flight up to occupational therapy. The room looks more like a workshop than a hospital department. There are workbenches, vises, numerous tools, piles of plywood and cut lumber, hand-printing presses, and looms. My therapist is Miss Miles, a tall, plain woman in her late twenties with an acne-scarred face.

We have built a birdhouse, but not a relationship—which is more my fault than hers. I don't like OT, which seems to me to be for people who are going to have difficulty finding occupations. I'm going to be a lawyer or go into politics. I know that by pulling down the printing press by hand to make my own stationery or pounding in nails to make a birdhouse that I am using muscles and redeveloping dexterity, but it's boring and certainly not occupational, unless it means occupying time that I could spend getting more PT.

On this day I don't want to weave a pot holder. "Can you teach me to be independent?" I ask Miss Miles.

"What do you mean?"

"I want to be able to bathe myself, dress myself, so I can go off to college and be on my own."

"I was thinking about starting that next week," she says.

"I'd like to start today."

She shows me how to move from wheelchair to bed and back. I'm just getting the hang of it when the hour ends. For the first time, I'm reluctant to leave OT. I usually spend the half hour before lunch on my own, practicing in the parallel bars or turning the captain's wheel. Now I stay and practice buttoning my shirt. My right hand is practically useless, but Miss Miles, who has foregone her own lunch to help me, shows me how to use a closed right fist to help the left fingers. I wonder if this technique would work putting on the condom.

After lunch, I return to PT and a second session on the table for range-of-motion exercises. Then Mrs. Walsh applies ice to try to stimulate select muscles. This is followed by a short walk in the tank, manned by Gresham, a fast-talking, cigar-chomping black man. Moving is certainly easier in here. I hold onto a pair of metal bars and, without benefit of the brace, manage to drag my right leg like the character Chester on *Gunsmoke*. I have a theory that if Gresham lowered the water an inch every day, I wouldn't notice the difference. As the water is about three and a half feet high, I figure that in about six weeks I'd be walking as well in an empty tank as I am in this full one.

My father is going to pick me up on his way home from work. I spend the rest of the afternoon in OT practicing transfers. Miss Miles also puts a device on the right wheel of my chair that makes it easier for me to push. She seems much nicer.

In the car, Dad tells me that he has commissioned the carpenter who built our tree house to build a set of parallel bars for the backyard. "That way you'll be able to practice your walking on the weekends," he explains. "And maybe you really won't have to go to Northwestern." Mom bent his ear today, no doubt.

"I was thinking I could also start trying to swim at Bud and Ruth's," I say. My aunt and uncle have a small pool in their backyard about fifteen minutes from our house.

Weston's call this morning woke all of us up, but especially me. I'm still a long way from New Haven. I have less than 150 days to get myself ready.

After dinner and TV and a visit from Julie Foster, a friend on the yearbook staff, Dad wheels me to the bedroom. He and Mom then walk Julie to her car. As they come back into the house, they discuss the best way to get me into bed. They are still talking outside my door when I accomplish the transfer all by myself. When they finally enter, I am under the covers, pretending to be asleep. The smile on my face gives me away.

.   .   .

"What's so funny?" Julie asks. Three weeks have passed since the night I first got into bed by myself.

"Nothing," I say. I'm not going to confess that I'm giggling because this is the first time I've ever slept with a girl—and that this isn't exactly the way I envisioned it. For example, I didn't think we'd be in a hospital bed with automatic controls for raising the head and feet.

Actually, we aren't *in* the bed, we are *on top* of it. But we are going to sleep together. Unfortunately, that's sleep as in "sleep," not as in "making love."

We are each fully clothed. Julie in blue jeans and a sleeveless white cotton shirt. Me in blue bell-bottoms and a Cubs T-shirt.

It's 3 A.M., and we have just returned from the city, where we celebrated my high school graduation (Julie is a junior) by seeing the Fifth Dimension perform at the College Inn, a nightclub in the Sherman House hotel. It's so late that it doesn't make sense for Julie to go home. In six hours, Bill and Larry and their girlfriends will pick us up, and we'll drive to the Playboy Club resort in Lake Geneva, Wisconsin, ninety minutes to the north.

Julie and I have just changed out of our graduation night duds into these informal clothes for the trip—out of sight from one another, of course. Earlier tonight, Julie wore a long pink formal. I wore a white tux and black pants and a ruffled white shirt. Weston, who accompanied us on our night on the town, forsook his usual white T-shirt for a white shirt with buttons and a dark suit. When we had posed for pictures, Jim had said, "You guys make quite a threesome."

I stifle a yawn. It's been a long day, beginning with the graduation ceremony itself, which took forever because our class is so large. I was easy to pick out in the crowd, however. I was the only graduate in a wheelchair.

I had hoped to accept my diploma on two feet. A week before the ceremony, I had asked Mrs. Walsh if I could try walking with crutches. "I'm feeling pretty comfortable in the parallel bars," I'd said. She had agreed that I was progressing nicely, but she told me I was a few weeks away from even trying crutches. "We don't want you to take a tumble," she explained.

When I complained about this to Bill, he remembered that he had an old pair of wooden crutches in his basement from the time he had broken his leg. He brought them over, and with Weston in front of me and Jim and Dad on each side of me, I tried to take my first steps outside the bar. I could move my left leg without much difficulty, but even with the brace, my right leg refused to advance more than a couple of inches—not far enough to get me anywhere. On graduation night, the crutches were only good for helping me stay on my feet for the pictures Dad took of me and Julie—and Weston.

Since I wasn't walking, New Trier decided that it would be easier if I skipped the graduation processional and waited on stage in my wheelchair for the presentation of diplomas. "Tough break," said a friend. "Now you won't get the money." The senior class boys always had a pool that paid big bucks to the guy who ended up paired on the graduation march with the least attractive girl in the class. In June of 1968, a dwarf was my sensitive classmates' unanimous selection. As my friend noted, since I was only four feet tall in the wheelchair, I would have been certain to be opposite the dwarf in the line.

As the procession began, I realized that I had been relegated to observer for more than just the graduation ceremony. I had not only missed classes and yearbook and debate activities, but all the fun that comes with being a second-semester senior: ditching school to go to Opening Day at Wrigley Field; late weeknights out because you've already been accepted at college; weekends with no curfew in the name of practicing for the freedom of college.

As one of my classmates received his diploma, he pumped a fist in the air and shouted, "Sex, drugs, rock and roll." I'd have settled for two out of three. Some of my classmates had experimented with pot and speed during the year. I wouldn't have gone for that, just like I had never gone for drinking. Being out of control was not my idea of fun. On the other hand, things had also progressed on the sexual front for many of my friends. That would have been fine with me.

There hadn't been any opportunities for that since December 6. Until this very moment with Julie on the bed, I hadn't even been in a private situation with a girl. My parents, my friends, and my caregivers were always moving in and out of my room at the hospital, the family room, even the room we were in right now.

Julie takes the side of the bed by the wall; I take the outside. She's an attractive brunette with a great sense of humor. Unless she's on a mission of mercy, she must feel that I'm cool enough to be seen with. That's almost enough to make me forget the disappointment in not being able to walk tonight—and to forget Randi.

"Thanks," I say.

"For what?"

"Just for coming along."

She seems surprised that I'm so grateful. "It was fun," she says. She gives me a kiss on the forehead—the first we have exchanged—then turns over to fall asleep. On my back, six inches from her, I struggle to move closer.

It's just like being on Mrs. Walsh's therapy table. I can't turn all the way onto my side. I try to roll over toward her, rocking my stronger left side to gain momentum. Like an auto stuck in an icy rut, I rock back and forth, from forward to reverse, until I finally get loose. Too much! Unable to hit the brakes, I slam Julie into the wall. She jumps.

"I just wanted to kiss you," I say.

She smiles, pushes me back on my back and then moves the top half of her body over mine. I kiss her furiously, all the unspent energy stored all these months moving to my lips and tongue. I try to move my hand to her breast, but I'm pinned. Shit! I'm obviously not destined ever to win a wrestling match.

Her mouth gives out first. "Now let's get some sleep," she says.

I don't want to stop. But she is asleep in an instant, and I can't rouse her. "Wake up. Wake up. Wake up," I whisper until it is loud enough to draw a visit from our curious dog. I cough. I "accidentally" hit the button on the hospital bed. I slurp some water. But Julie is out for the night.

I'm just about to close my eyes when I feel a familiar but long-absent aching in my groin. I reach down and feel the growing bulge. For the first time since the accident, I have a spontaneous hard-on. I encourage its growth with my hand. *Wake up. Wake up. Wake up.* And it obliges.

CHAPTER 8

"Yo, bro."

It took me a minute to realize that I was "bro." The black man with the red Afro was talking to me, the white boy with the short brown hair. We did have a couple of things in common: we were both in green wheelchairs and we were both waiting for our physical therapists.

"What happened to you, bro?"

"Hurt myself wrestling," I said.

"Car here," he said. "Drove my Camaro through a telephone pole." He pivoted his chair and glided effortlessly toward me, thanks to forearms that were as massive as his legs were thin.

Paraplegic, I thought.

"I used to rassle," he said. He looked me over. "What weight were you?"

The correct answer was: "Oh, I didn't wrestle on a team. This was just in gym class." But somehow it sounded more manly to let him believe that I'd been hurt in competition. "One fifty-two," I lied.

"One seventy-seven here," he said.

It was late July. I had been coming to the Rehab for almost three months. This was the longest, most substantive conversation I'd had with any patient except for the day Bobby Kennedy was shot.

Henry Betts had been Joseph Kennedy's doctor after the family patriarch had suffered a stroke. When I had arrived at the institute on the morning of June 5, there were rumors that Bobby would be coming for rehabilitation if he lived. "First Dr. King, now this," lamented an older man, a former English professor whose leg had been amputated because of complications from diabetes. He asked if I knew the term "pathetic fallacy." When I said I didn't, he talked about famous works in which the protagonist's life falls to ruin as the world itself collapses. I knew what he was getting at, but I didn't choose to put myself in this story line. My life was not falling to ruin. I had pictured working for Kennedy and joining the White House staff in 1972, if not next January.

The ex-wrestler with the Afro continued talking. "That your valet?" he asked, pointing at Weston.

I frowned. "Nurse," I said.

I was embarrassed. My liberal Jewish parents had raised me well enough to feel guilty about being a "have" when there were still "have-nots" around the corner. Valet. Nurse. Chauffeur. It didn't matter what I called Weston. The fact of the matter was that because the Fiffers were well-off, I was making this journey first-class. My inquisitor and most of the rest of the patients at the Rehab were going coach—or even baggage.

I had often teased my father—sometimes lightheartedly, sometimes nastily—when he acquired and displayed symbols of material comfort, a Patek Philipe watch, or a Cadillac, for God's sake. Shortly after I had been hurt, I had noticed that he was wearing a new ring—a gold number, thick as the bands on the expensive, long, fat, burgundy-colored imported cigars he had started smoking.

"That's sick," I said from my Circolectric bed. "There are people starving, and you buy a gold ring? It's disgusting to have that much money."

"That money has bought you round-the-clock nursing, the best doctors. I don't hear you complaining about that," he replied.

He had me there. I had *never* complained about or refused any perks associated with financial comfort before the accident—camp, vacations, various lessons—and I certainly hadn't complained about post-accident advantages like specialists and nurse-valets. Despite my posturing, I would have been horrified if Dad had stood up at the dinner table and announced that he had given all of his (that's our) money to charity and that henceforth we would lead a much less comfortable, privileged life.

Having money was making it easier for me to overcome my injury. Certainly, being affluent allowed me to get the best care. But being affluent also gave me a greater incentive to overcome the injury. Not because I had extra drive to recover so I could enjoy the upper-middle-class life, but because I felt guilty that my life had been so easy to date. I may not have known the term "pathetic fallacy," but I had done enough reading of literature, history, and the daily newspapers to realize that even the blessed (like the Kennedys) eventually face hardship. So I accepted my injury—trying not to dwell on why it had happened, but looking at it instead as the challenge which would define me for the rest of my life. It was an opportunity to prove myself.

Sir Edmund Hillary had Tenzing Norgay when he became the first to climb Mt. Everest. I had Weston. Having help didn't diminish the challenge Hillary or I faced, nor did it negate our accomplishments. You could call Weston my Sherpa if you wanted, but I was proud of my progress. I was pushing myself to the limits and extending those limits every day.

"What you need your own nurse for?" the man continued. Mrs. Walsh's entrance saved me from the interrogation. She told me to take a lap around the floor on my crutches, and told the man—she called him Harmon—to wheel over to the big exercise mat.

I stood up. Weston, who had been sitting a few seats over, handed me the crutches the Rehab had finally issued me in early July. Unlike the wooden ones that I had been surreptitiously practicing on at home, these Canadian crutches were made of metal and, thanks to hinged cuffs, were worn comfortably around the wrists rather than uncomfortably in the armpits. A short padded grip extended at a right angle from each pole. The dire predictions of Dr. Graham notwithstanding, I was walking fairly well with these devices. My right hand and arm were just strong enough to allow me to grasp and move the right crutch, and my braced right leg was finally strong enough to keep up with the left one.

I started my lap. Ignoring Mrs. Walsh's instructions, Harmon followed me down the hall. "Bro, what you doin' with a wheelchair? If I could walk like you, I wouldn't be messin' with no motherfuckin' chair."

That night I told Dad to put the motherfuckin' chair in the basement (although not in those words). A few days later, we gave Weston his walking papers. I could get myself dressed and up and about now. I didn't need a nurse anymore; I just needed a driver to take me to RIC at nine and pick me up at five. I had a summer job just like the rest of my friends: mine was spending eight hours a day getting myself in shape to go to New Haven. (I worked overtime evenings on the parallel bars at home and on the weekends in my aunt and uncle's pool.) Dad hired a graduate student from Northwestern to be my chauffeur.

. . .

As my job neared its end and my departure for college approached, I looked around for Harmon, whom I hadn't seen for several weeks. Just as Dr. Graham's words behind my back had pushed me to the next level, so, too, had this man's words to my face. I wanted to thank him.

I finally saw him on my very last day at the Rehab. He wasn't sitting in his wheelchair. Instead, he lay stomach down on a four-wheeled cart, his torso swathed in a white sheet.

"What's up, bro?" he said.

"I'm going to college tomorrow," I said. "I came to say goodbye to everybody. I haven't seen you for a while."

"No shit. Got me a motherfuckin' bedsore on my ass wouldn't heal. They had to take me by the hospital to get a graft. I gotta be on this motherfuckin' cart 'til that motherfucker heals." He pushed his cart closer to me. "Where you going to college, bro? I had some schools write me about rassling, but I went to 'Nam instead."

"I'm going to Yale," I said.

"Ain't never heard of that school. Where it at?"

I was shocked. Elitist that I was, I thought everyone had heard of Yale. "It's in New Haven, Connecticut."

"Well, fine. You do good out there, you hear." He extended a right hand still far stronger than mine. We shook, and then he wheeled off. He stopped a few seconds later and turned his cart back in my direction. "Hey, bro," he said, "you ain't taking no valet with you, right?"

"Right," I smiled.

I had been practicing my skills for independent living with Miss Miles for weeks. In mid-August, I'd had a dry run. Mom and Dad felt comfortable enough taking Jim and Tommy and heading up to Toronto for a long weekend—the family's first vacation since my accident. They left me at home in the care of Bill and Larry. We promised that there would be no wild parties and no drinking.

None of us were drinkers, so I was mildly offended when I noticed that they had removed the key from its usual place in the liquor cabinet. I guessed where they'd hidden it, opened the cabinet, and wrote a note chiding them for not trusting us. Then the four of us proceeded to drink. Water.

Dr. Levine wanted me drinking ten glasses a day to keep my kidneys flushed. Larry said he didn't think that sounded difficult. Our pal Nemo agreed. So when we sat down to play cards, I insisted that we forget about our penny-nickel-dime ante rules and play "water poker." Each time you stayed in until the end of a hand and lost, you had to drink a glass of water.

After about half an hour, I noticed that all bluffing had ceased and my pals were folding rather than risking holding out and losing. The next morning Larry complained that he had been up to go to the bathroom three times overnight. "Join the club," I said. I hadn't slept through the night since the accident—at first because of the trauma, but now because of my high water intake.

Bill and Larry had a softball game the next afternoon, and I tagged along. Sitting in the first row of the peeling wooden stands, struggling just to keep my back up so my chest wouldn't be sucked into my knees, I watched the team I was supposed to have pitched for. They wore purple jerseys with SHERMAN CARTAGE on the front in yellow lettering, and yellow

numbers and nicknames on the back: "TEETH," "SOL," "MR.
CUB JR." My own jersey—number 7 after Mickey Mantle—
would have read FIFE.

I missed sports. Sometimes when I was alone, I'd throw a
hip into the wall, a shoulder into the door. I missed contact,
and I missed competition.

I could rationalize that my physical therapy was the ultimate in sports—the relentless training of the body to perform
to the best of its ability, the constant testing of the human machine against such opponents as gravity, spasticity, and atro-
phy. Trying to manuever on crutches was, I could argue,
sportlike. My concentration, my endurance, agility—all essential for success in athletic competition—were all essential now
just to keep me on my feet.

The constant concentrating drained my energy faster than
the act of walking itself, particularly in crowds. Crowd walking was my equivalent of the slalom—body and crutches
working in unison, speeding up, slowing down, lifting the
crutches to avoid the people and stay on the course.

The softball game was almost over when a young athlete I'd
never seen approached me. Blue-jerseyed, cleats and glove in
hand, he said, "One of our guys didn't show up. Would you
like to play?"

I declined without explanation. Maybe my walking and physical therapy fell under the definition of sport, but as the kid in
the blue jersey said, you *play* sports. Therapy wasn't playing.

That night, we had a party. There were girls, but it wasn't
wild—at least not for me. Bill's girlfriend Susan came, as did
Larry's girlfriend Jennifer. I had tried to reach Julie. She had
been away for most of the summer, but she'd been back two
weeks and hadn't returned any of my calls.

First Randi. Now Julie. Before the accident, plenty of girls had given me the cold shoulder, and I'd left my share of girls twisting in the wind after promising I'd phone. I'd survived and so had the girls, no doubt. But now my ego was as fragile as my neck. Each slight made me question my manhood. Each unreturned call made me think I wasn't normal.

Bill and Larry slipped off with their girls while I tried to persuade my neighbor Billy Biederman that the Supremes were far superior to the Doors. My heart wasn't in the debate. I wanted to be off making out or getting laid. I knew that some of my friends had gone all the way, but I hadn't even come close. I remembered one evening before the accident when a girl with a reputation for being pretty loose had encouraged me to go further as I lay on top of her on a couch in her basement. I'd felt guilty. I didn't really like her that much and would have been uncomfortable presenting her to anyone as my date. So I hadn't gone any further. I hadn't regretted it at the time, but I did now.

After the party, Bill and I were the last two awake. We'd slept over at each other's houses scores of times, double-dated just as often. When he'd come to Florida with our family, the two of us had our own room. I had spent more time with him than anyone other than my parents and Jim. But our conversations were rarely self-revelatory—unless they revealed that I wasn't the self-revealing kind of teenager. I didn't feel the need for words with him. We were kind of like White Sox shortstop Luis Aparicio and second baseman Nellie Fox: we knew each other inside out and were there for each other without having to say much. We revealed our characters to one another on the baseball diamond or the basketball court or the hockey rink or the soccer field. (I'd add the golf course, but it would probably be more accurate to say the golf cart.)

As he cleaned up in the family room, Bill surprised me by asking how I felt about getting hurt. "Like, we're best friends, and you've never told me how you feel," he said.

I took a drink of water to give myself time to frame the right response. "I haven't told anyone how I feel," I said. "I don't like to analyze things, at least not this."

Bill put down the empty Coke cans he was holding and sat on a kitchen chair. "Why not?"

"It seems to me that the more you think about something like this, the more you get into trouble. I think I've survived by not thinking as much as possible."

"Just sweep it under the rug?" he asked.

"Yep. And maybe next time you look it'll be all gone."

I realized that I wasn't being completely honest. I'd had so much time alone, unable to move, that all I could do was analyze. One of the conclusions I'd drawn was that those who cared about me had, in some ways, suffered more than I had emotionally over the last eight months—because they could only guess what I was thinking, how I was feeling. I seemed to be the same old cocky, unflappable Steve. But was it a front? Had my psyche remained (like the rest of me) a virgin through this ordeal? I knew they put themselves in my shoes and couldn't imagine surviving something like this.

Bill deserved an answer. "I think I was unlucky to get hurt," I said carefully, "but that since then I've been pretty lucky and that pretty soon everything is gonna be like it was. I'm proud of my family and myself, and I think I'm a better person because of what happened, you know, my character, but I wouldn't wish this on anyone as a way to build character. I think that as long as I keep improving every day, I'm not going to worry."

"I don't think I would have been strong enough to handle something like this," Bill said.

"I don't think you know until it happens," I said. "And I hope you never find out."

After my parents returned from Toronto, we all met with Miss Miles and made a checklist of every step I would have to take from the moment I woke up until I went to sleep again. Showering. Putting on my leg bag. Dressing. Tying my shoes. Meals. Carrying books and papers to class. Getting to class.

If the bad news was that only one of my hands was functional, the good news was it was my left hand. I hadn't had to train my right hand to do all the tasks I had done with the left for seventeen years. I just had to train the widowed hand to do everything its departed partner had helped with in the past— buttoning shirts, tying ties, tying shoelaces.

Miss Miles had been very helpful. She replaced top buttons with Velcro. She found pre-knotted ties that clipped easily onto my collar. She provided No-Bowz, tiny cubes that allowed me to secure my shoelaces one-handed. And she suggested that we put zippers in the inseams of my pants so that I could change—either for reasons of fashion or necessity (leaky leg bag)—without having to go through the difficult process of taking off my shoes and putting them back on.

While she was working on these small but essential solutions, Dad was trying to solve the biggest potential problem: getting around the campus. I was walking, but I didn't have the strength or stamina to negotiate the required distances in good weather, much less in winter. I would need some kind of vehicle. Driving a car was out. Yale didn't lend itself to automobiles because many classes were inside quadrangles well off the street. Besides, my right foot wasn't strong enough to press the accelerator. Motorcycles and mopeds were also out; I couldn't mount them.

Dad took a day off from work, and we visited several showrooms. We stopped first at a dealership featuring all-terrain vehicles. Despite its name, the vehicle was not appropriate for the terrain I would be facing. It was too big and heavy. It also looked like a tank—not exactly the right fashion statement to make as Vietnam protest intensified.

At stop two, we looked at golf carts. We were getting warmer. This vehicle would do if we couldn't find anything better.

We did find something better. It was called an E-Z-GO—a shiny yellow three-wheeled cart designed to transport workers within a factory. About half the size of a golf cart, it was versatile and sturdy enough to drive on sidewalks or streets. The accelerator was broad enough so that I could press with my left foot, but I couldn't reach the brake. No problem, said the dealer. He'd have his mechanic customize a hand brake. He also said he'd put long tubes in the back for crutch storage. Everything was falling into place.

Except on the home front. Bill's parents had invited our family and Larry's family to a dinner celebrating our pending departures to college. It was to start at seven o'clock. Seven arrived, but Dad didn't. We called his office. No answer. We waited fifteen minutes, then called again. No answer. We left a message for him and then headed to Bill's house. We called the law firm from there. Still no answer.

Bill's parents and my parents had been friends for years. My parents and Larry's parents were only casual acquaintances. Mom and I didn't know whether to be worried or embarrassed by Dad's unexplained absence. At eight, we suggested that dinner be served.

Dad arrived half an hour later, as we were digging into Mrs. Solomon's veal parmigiana. He teetered to the table and kissed my mother on the cheek. Then he addressed us all: "Sorry, I'm late. Been a rough day. A really rough day." He slurred his words. He was smashed.

For the next hour, he dominated the conversation. But very little he said made any sense. I had never seen him like this. I didn't want to crawl in a hole so much as I wanted to punch him out.

Bill's parents and Larry's parents acted as if nothing were wrong. I shifted uncomfortably in my seat, unwilling to establish eye contact with my friends, unable to establish eye contact to chastise my drunken father. Mom finally manufactured an excuse for an early exit; we needed to get home to do some packing for the trip to New Haven. Dad refused Bill's father's offer to drive him home. We followed his car to make sure he arrived safely.

Then I lit into him. "I can't believe this," I said, as he wobbled in the family room door. "I have never been so embarrassed in my life. You made a fool of yourself and of me in front of my friends and their parents. You spoiled the party."

Dad collapsed into a chair. "I'm sorry, Stevo."

"Why would you do that? This was an important night for me and Bill and Larry. You stink."

"Let me explain."

"I don't want to hear an explanation."

Dad rose unsteadily to his feet. "I hope you never have a day like I had today."

"I hope you never have a night like I had tonight," I countered.

He explained that he and his law partners had met at lunchtime to determine compensation for the coming year. This was always a difficult proposition, but this year it had become particularly problematic and acrimonious. If each lawyer received what he thought he deserved, the firm would be substantially in the red. No one would budge. As senior partner, he was the target of much of the frustration. After six hours of nonstop bickering, he had finally fashioned a compromise that everyone could live with. Then they all shook hands and went out and got drunk.

"Not good enough," I said. "I'll never forget this."

I gave him the silent treatment for the next twenty-four hours. Mom finally pulled me aside. "It's been a rough year for your dad."

"I don't care. He was wrong."

"He's had to be 'on duty' every minute since the accident. We all have. Maybe it's a good sign—a sign that he thinks you're well enough so he can go off duty for a little while. Why don't you give him a break."

It hadn't occurred to me that there might be such a reason for my father getting drunk. In my Ptolemaic universe, in which everything revolved around me, I hadn't considered that up to this point, in order to get and keep me on my feet, my parents had been forced to stay in control, to be on duty as much as I had to stay in control. Maybe it was a good sign that Dad finally felt he could let loose. The least I could do was give him a break.

.   .   .

After saying goodbye to Harmon at RIC, I head down the corridor to say my last farewell—this to Dr. Betts. Left crutch. Right foot. Right crutch. Left foot. Left crutch. Uh-oh! I'm suddenly yanked forward like a kid holding onto the leash of a runaway dog. I'm the china on the tablecloth pulled by a magician—a bad magician.

"Goddamnnnnnnnnnn."

A minute passes. I finally open my eyes. I'm lost—like when I've just awakened from an unscheduled nap. Who am I? Where am I? What time is it? What happened?

I don't know the answer to any of these questions. I know I

THREE QUARTERS, TWO DIMES, AND A NICKEL 115

am on a floor somewhere and that my head hurts and that a man dressed in white and a woman in a blue skirt and white blouse are standing over me. They look familiar. Do I know them?

"Steve, are you okay?" the woman asks. Now I recognize her—Miss Miles.

Snatches of fact are beginning to come back. I am Steve. I am at the Rehab Institute. I have fallen. "Fuck," I say. "Fuck. Fuck. Fuck." I try to roll over.

"Don't move," Miss Miles says. "You must have slipped on that patch of water by the drinking fountain."

I sure didn't see it. I thought I was using crutches, not divining rods.

Dr. Betts arrives.

"I know I'm supposed to be going somewhere tomorrow," I say. "But where?"

"To school," Miss Miles says. "To Yale."

I try to sit up.

"Stay where you are, Steve," Dr. Betts says. "We want to make sure your neck is okay."

My neck! Oh God. My head is on fire. "Fuck. Fuck. Fuck. Fuck." I put my hand to my mouth and come away with a palm full of blood.

The man in white—he's an orderly—bends down, picks something up, and hands it to Dr. Betts. "Here are his teeth."

My teeth! I reach into my mouth. My two front teeth are missing. "Oh God. Fuck. Fuck. Fuck."

Bill stands over me. He had driven me to the institute and then headed over to a tailor shop on Michigan Avenue to pick up my customized pants. "I'm sorry," he tells Dr. Betts. "I shouldn't have left him."

"It's my fucking fault, not yours," I say. How's that for honesty!

Dr. Betts calls my parents and supervises the taking of neck and back X-rays. The paramedics load me onto a stretcher and carry me out. An ambulance is to take me and the X-rays to Dr. Meyer's office in the suburbs. I am so embarrassed to be leaving the Rehab this way.

We wait for the elevator with a group of men and women in wheelchairs. "I feel sorry for him," says a young girl in between puffs on her portable respirator. She's a total quad, and she feels sorry for me?

Dr. Betts has called my dentist, who has instructed that the teeth—which fell out whole—be placed in a saline solution in the hope that they might be reimplanted later in the day.

Dr. Meyer agrees with Dr. Betts's assessment that there has been no damage to the neck. The fusion is still secure. But my head is still throbbing, and the ringing I hear won't go away. I try to stand. My legs buckle. Meyer puts me in a wheelchair— so much for my "never again" vow—and sends me back to the city and my dentist, Dr. Sondell.

"The teeth can be salvaged," says Dr. Sondell, a short, trim man in his sixties with thick black glasses. "I can stick them back in and then secure them with wire and a plastic shield. But we're going to have to keep your mouth sensate." He is wearing a camera around his neck.

My vocabulary is as bad as my balance. "What's sensate?" I ask.

"No painkiller, no anesthetic."

I consider myself tough because I refuse Novocain when getting fillings. But I don't know about this.

"I want to take some pictures first," says the dentist. "I'm sure one of the journals will be interested." He bounces around me like a fashion photographer, getting shots from all angles.

"Will I get royalties?"

The holes where the teeth had been are bloody red, pulpy. The dentist mates the two white teeth with their roots by shoving them up as far as possible. I think I feel his fingers all the way under my eyeballs. I have never experienced so much pain.

When it's over, Dr. Sondell hands me a mirror, then grabs his camera to take more pictures. For the first time, I see the damage. My face could qualify for disaster aid. My cheeks are puffed to twice their size, my lips raw, and a variety of lumps and welts make my jaw and chin look like a bas-relief map.

I go to the bathroom. I see myself in the full-size mirror and look upward. I flash God the finger. "Are you happy? You got the only part of me that you didn't get before. All I had left was above the neck. Are you happy?"

And then I whisper: "What did I do to deserve this? Will you please tell me? What the goddamn fuck did I do to deserve any of this?"

No answer.

My parents have planned a going-away party. A dozen friends are coming. Even though we've decided to delay heading East for at least a day, I don't want the party canceled. I eat Jell-O on the couch while my friends eat my favorite food, now forbidden—ribs. After dinner, we play poker. I joke that I'm sure to win because it looks like I have two of everything.

Two days later, the cheeks still puffed, the welts now half black, half yellow, like partially eclipsed suns, my parents and I fly East. We leave the wheelchair at home. I walk to the plane with pain and pride. My ears are still ringing. My teeth appear to be holding their own. It is nine months and one week since the accident. I feel like a newborn child.

CHAPTER 9

I am not difficult to spot as I cross the Old Campus, Yale's leafy, square-block quadrangle ringed by freshman halls and classrooms. Young men barefoot or sandaled, in blue jeans or cutoffs, toss baseballs or Frisbees, lug furniture or cases of beer. Wearing wing tip shoes and No-Bowz, short leg brace and leg bag hidden under plaid suit pants with zippers, I lug myself on crutches through these "peers," moving as quickly as possible. I'd like to withdraw from the sunlight, find a nice room inside where I can escape the suffocating feeling of freedom apparently able to be enjoyed by all but me.

At last I find Durfee, the hall where I am to live. But there are six steps up to the front door, six steep and narrow steps I cannot climb. It seems that the entire Old Campus stops to watch me try—my first college test—and I fail. If only there were a railing. I finally give up and lean on my father.

"Now isn't that stupid, to have given you a room up here," my mother says.

"We requested a first-floor room. That's what they gave me."

"They should have known we meant ground level."

My freshman counselor says that he will see if a railing can be installed. Bob Bissell, one of my assigned roommates, says that if not, he'll always be available to help.

Dad drives me to the Admissions Office to thank a counselor who had been particularly nice over the summer. There is a winding flight of stairs which I insist on climbing, but halfway up my legs lock. Dad has to get on his knees to break the spastic reaction.

"What the hell is going to happen in the winter?" my mother asks. "It's not too late to go to Stanford."

At least she didn't say Northwestern. All summer, all but a few of Mom and Dad's friends had advised against letting me leave home so soon after being injured. After I fell at the Rehab, the holdouts also urged that I stay home. I know it has taken a tremendous amount of courage for my parents to let me go halfway across the country just a few weeks after getting out of the wheelchair. Since my fall on my face hasn't scared them off, I can only conclude that they have a great deal of faith in me or that they really want to get rid of me!

After seeing the counselor, we drive to Student Health to check out the therapy department. The director of student health, Dr. Heatherton, is a tall man in his early sixties, bald and bony, with a nose that looks like a strung arrow. He has a big, cold office with a stone floor and walls that are bare except for a few diplomas and oil paintings of severe-looking Yale officials from the days when the university had a stronger religious connection. Heatherton pulls out my medical records and says, "You've had a remarkable recovery, Mr. Fiffer." He then informs me that my freshman counselor spoke to a dean, who spoke to him about my problem with the stairs at Durfee Hall. "You have been given a room in Timothy Dwight College," the doctor says.

Timothy Dwight and Yale's eleven other residential colleges are inhabited exclusively by sophomores, juniors, and seniors. Freshmen are assigned to the colleges, but live on the Old Campus.

"But I want to live with my classmates," I say, explaining that one of my high school friends has a room on the Old Campus that is literally at ground level. "Maybe I could live with him," I suggest.

"Young man," Dr. Heatherton replies sternly, "don't ever forget that you are here only by our good graces. If you want to remain, you shall play the game by our rules. And if you can't make it on your own, I'm afraid you will have to go back home." Later my parents will report that he told them he didn't expect me to last beyond the first semester.

Unlike the Gothic-styled Old Campus, Timothy Dwight College—which everyone calls "TD"—is built in the colonial fashion, and its courtyard is considerably smaller and quieter than the freshman grounds. My new room sits in a corner of the college, three blocks away from my old room and from the 999 other members of the Class of 1972. This room is also up six stairs, but they are inside the doorway, not outside, and there is a railing.

We rent a hospital bed and a water cooler. Mom insists that the Yale-issue bed also remain so that Bob and my two other assigned Old Campus roommates can stay over if they wish. Over my objections, Dad hires a senior to look in on me each morning.

As Mom gets the room in order, Dad and I spend the next two days checking out classes, walking to some, riding in the rental car to others. Yale was founded in 1701, and it seems that most of the buildings were built only shortly thereafter. There are steps leading up to the entrance, steps leading from the entrance

to the foyer, and, finally, stairways upon stairways. The political
science course I want to take is three steep flights up. Anthropology is only a few steps up from ground level. Anthropology
it is. Couldn't some rich alum have donated elevators?

Couldn't we have sued? My father was a lawyer, but he
never considered legal action to make Yale's classrooms and
living quarters accessible. This was a time when few people
asked for or expected special treatment because of disability,
race, or gender. It wasn't Yale's responsibility to adapt to me,
we all agreed. It was my job to adapt to Yale or, as Dr.
Heatherton said, go elsewhere.

My mother flies back home after four days. Dad stays to
wait for the E-Z-GO, which arrives two days later. The New
Haven police and the campus police each say that I can drive
in the street and on sidewalks, but I must wear a helmet at all
times. As I slowly pull out from beneath the red brick archway
of TD to the street for my first test drive, Dad runs behind the
cart like a dog chasing a car, barking instructions.

It has taken six days to create my world. On the seventh
day, Dad returns to Chicago instead of resting. When he and
Mom call that night, I politely tell them everything is fine. Bob
and I have already become good friends. I'm spending time on
the Old Campus in my high school pal's accessible room. I like
my classes. And I've arranged to see my old Cherubs girlfriend
Pat, who now attends Connecticut College, about forty-five
minutes away. When my parents call the next night, I tell them
to stop checking up on me and inform them that I have dismissed my student helper; I don't need him. When they call for
the third night in a row, I hang up on them.

On my fourth day on my own, I head across campus for a
speech by Mark Rudd, the leader of the Columbia University
chapter of Students for a Democratic Society, the radical group

that held the dean of that school hostage in May. The only thing I am interested in taking to the streets is my E-Z-GO, but I am interested in hearing what Rudd has to say.

I float to the sky and see myself strap on my helmet, start the E-Z-GO, and cruise out onto Temple Street, then Wall Street, then onto Church. Suddenly, I am in the middle of a parade. "Mexican Independence Day," yells a comely young woman from the back seat of the convertible in front of me. A band is marching behind me, playing music with a pulsating Latin rhythm.

"Where did you come from?" shouts a boy from the curb. There are drum majors and baton twirlers and flags and streamers and I am in the middle of it all. The procession turns onto Grove Street past the north flank of my residence. Scores of my dormmates are hanging out their windows. They cheer when they see me. I flash the peace sign, then wave.

Where have I come from? A long way. I've earned this parade, the applause. *I'm* independent, too. I drop from the sky back into my body. I feel great. I don't want to miss this because I'm off somewhere floating.

.   .   .

Dr. Heatherton had placed me in the liver-spotted hands of the Student Health Department's senior therapists, the O'Malley brothers. Had I been Calvin Hill, the star running back on Yale's football team, I suspect that I would have had no complaints about Kenny O'Malley, who was pushing sixty-five, and his brother Timmy, who was a year or two his junior. These affable gentlemen, who had started in the rehabilitation field by taping ankles for Yale's powerhouse football teams in the 1930s, were no doubt competent at nursing bumps and bruises, even sprains and tears. But they had absolutely no idea how to treat someone with a spinal cord injury.

My half-hour sessions with them followed a predictably disappointing, if comical, course. I would come in, find an empty cubicle, and start to take off my shoes and brace. Then, Kenny, a dead ringer for the actor Pat O'Brien, would enter and insist on helping. I indulged him. My shoes finally off, he would help me up on the exercise table and then—and this happened like clockwork—excuse himself to go to the bathroom. "Can't drink coffee like I used to," he would say with a smile.

But he didn't go to the bathroom. I could hear him talking in the hallway with his brother. Timmy's counsel was always the same: "Take him through the range of motion, Ken."

So back he would come, a sense of purpose on his face, and sure enough, he took me through the range of motion. As he helped move my arms or legs, he told me Yale football stories. Larry Kelley, the Heisman Trophy winner in 1936 was pigeon-toed. Clinton Frank, the winner in 1937, had the biggest ankles he ever taped.

Range of motion done—this took all of five minutes—Kenny was off again. Several minutes later, his brother would appear. A dead ringer for Kenny except that he had a full head of white hair, Timmy would ask, "Well, what should we do now?"

"How about icing my quadriceps or giving me active resistance," I would say as calmly as possible. Like a jailhouse lawyer, I had learned enough about my predicament to prosecute my appeal.

"I know," Timmy would reply with a wide grin, and I couldn't hate him for it, "how about range of motion?"

By November, I was supplementing these daily debacles with thrice weekly trips to the Yale Natatorium. There, a six-foot-four, 250-pound, bald, sixty-year-old Russian émigré named Walt lowered me into the water, handed me a Styrofoam board, and dragged me the length of the pool, then again, and again, and again—one hundred meters in all. "Keeck, keeck," he exhorted in his thick East European accent. These laps done, he clambered out of the pool and followed along the deck as I backstroked another hundred meters. "Poosh it, poosh it," he would yell.

Returning to my room exhausted, I often fell asleep at my desk before dinner while studying—a state of affairs I attributed to the workout, not the homework. I was enjoying my classes, particularly an English survey course taught by Professor A. Bartlett Giamatti and others. My course instructor allowed us pompous freshmen great leeway. He tolerated, even praised, papers in which I would eschew the assigned topic to, say, compare Ibsen's Master Builder to President Lyndon Baines Johnson. (Vietnam informed much of our academic and social discourse, and most of us were vocal in our opposition to the war. But our protest did not become violent that year as it did at other schools—in part because we were under the moral and political influence of the campus's most prominent antiwar activist, University Chaplain William Sloane Coffin, and in part because there was a feel-good atmosphere on campus that made it hard to get angry. This atmosphere was generated by, of all things, an undefeated football team so good that it was actually ranked in the top twenty nationally and by a mesmerizing new Yale Daily News comic strip by a junior named Garry Trudeau, featuring an undergrad named Mike Doonesbury.)

If I was still asleep at dinnertime, one of the sophomores from down the hall or one of my freshman friends from the Old Campus would wake me up on his way to the Timothy

Dwight College dining hall. I say "his" without reservation because there were no female undergraduates at Yale when I entered. Our Class of 1972 was the last all-male class admitted
to an institution that was already in the midst of dramatic
change. Nineteen sixty-eight was the first year that the school
didn't require students to wear coats and ties to meals and, I
was told, the first year that students were allowed to have
women in their rooms with the doors closed (not that this rule
had ever been universally observed).

Nineteen sixty-eight was also the year of the Great Experiment. When students lobbied for the most dramatic change of
all—the admission of women—Yale President Kingman Brew-
ster handled the issue with his usual diplomacy. To determine
whether the school was ready to go coed, he invited women
from various Seven Sister schools to live on campus for a week
and attend classes. The institution and the coeds survived, and
the Class of 1973 was opened to women (although not at the
expense of Yale's expressed commitment to "produce 1,000
male leaders a year"). Our class and those above us accepted
a limited number of female transfers.

Looking back, I wonder if the accident hadn't left me a little touched. What was I thinking about in even applying to a
school without women? I can only say that my prematricula-
tion conversations with graduates from my high school already in New Haven persuaded me that girls flocked to Yale
on the weekends. This proved true—even after coeducation.
Buses from Smith, Wellesley, Mount Holyoke, Vassar, Connecticut College, Briarcliffe, and any number of other schools
brought hundreds of women to Friday and Saturday mixers
hosted by the residential colleges.

These mixers featured live bands and unlimited beer. Unfortunately, still precarious (and self-conscious) on my crutches, I

didn't feel comfortable dancing or drinking. "No thanks, I'm walking," became my standard line when offered a foamy cup of Bud or Schlitz. Many of my fellow freshmen shared my shyness in approaching women to dance, but few were timid at the tap. Drunk or sober, they often ended up in my room by evening's end pouring out their souls about unrequited love, or fathers who didn't understand them, or the meaninglessness of their lives.

Soon these sessions had spilled over to weeknights, too, as everyone knew that I would be studying in my room rather than at the library. Room 1594, Timothy Dwight College, became something of a salon, but rather than being Gertrude Stein, I was Ann Landers. My new friends seemed to believe that I was the one with the answers to their troubles with girls, parents, professors.

I was a good listener (the accident hadn't affected my ears), but I'm not sure how good an adviser I was. My counsel was always the same: "It's not that serious. Don't let it bother you. Things will work out for the best."

"Why does everyone come to me?" I asked Bob Bissell, who had become my best friend at Yale.

"You have an incredibly healthy perspective on things," he said.

Did I? Or, because of the accident, did I have no perspective at all? (Some people saw the glass as half empty, others half full. I saw it as four more ounces needed to flush my kidneys.)

I wasn't having any trouble with my parents or professors, but I didn't get off on the right foot with girls. I had hoped to resume my relationship with my Cherubs sweetheart Pat. She visited early in the fall, and we spent a pleasant evening talking, but when I called a few days later to invite her back for the coming weekend, she said she was busy. She was busy the next weekend, too.

We had been such a hot couple two summers earlier. What could have happened to cool her off? It had to be the accident. I wrote her an angry letter chastising her for judging me by my "temporary physical appearance." She wrote me back an equally angry letter, chastising me for judging her so wrongly. The truth was, she was truly busy—visiting her boyfriend from high school, who now went to Harvard. She offered to fix me up with one of her classmates, a girl named Lonnie.

Lonnie was sweet. She seemed to like me (enough to take off everything but her panties for a lengthy romp on the hospital bed only two hours after she arrived). Unfortunately, she had a plain face, an overbite, and lifeless brown hair. I was looking for someone more attractive. Had I been counseling myself as well as I apparently counseled others, I might have said: "You fool. You don't want to be judged by your looks. How can you judge others by theirs?" But I wasn't offering myself such counsel (nor was I likely to accept it), so I continued my search for a trophy girlfriend.

I knew I wasn't going to find this beauty at a mixer. Not because she wasn't there, but because I didn't feel confident trying to make a positive first impression on strangers at these dances by lumbering over on my crutches. I did, however, feel confident that I could win over most any girl who got to know me over the phone first. So I badgered new college friends and old high school friends at nearby schools for the phone numbers of pretty women whom I could woo invisibly with wit and self-efacement. While the wit was spontaneous, the self-effacement was studied. In each conversation I waited for the appropriate time to announce quite matter-of-factly that I was temporarily on crutches.

Why? the girl on the other end would invariably inquire.

Because I had been hurt while wrestling in high school. (As always, I took great pains to give the impression that the injury had taken place during a varsity match, rather than a gym class.)

What kind of accident?

Broken neck. Total paralysis. Doctors said I'd never walk again. (Delivered to convey that I didn't consider this a big deal, so she shouldn't either.)

As a result of this act, I had as many dates during my first year as most of my friends. The girls were often pretty, but none of the relationships were memorable or worth repeating. I'm sure the feeling was mutual. Case in point: Babby P., a well-built, chestnut-haired senior at a nearby prep school. When she took out her contact lenses at the end of a long, boring evening, I joked, "You look much better without them." Without batting an eyelash, she shot back: "So do you." We never saw each other again.

.   .   .

I observed the one-year anniversary of my accident shortly before returning home for winter break. It was not a particularly happy occasion. I had been certain that the dramatic progress of the past spring and summer would continue into the fall, but it hadn't. Going about my daily life was certainly easier than when I had arrived in New Haven. However, I attributed this to my mental ability to solve problems rather than any major physical gains. I did notice that I could get out of certain chairs which had earlier posed problems and that I didn't tire as quickly as before, but the fingers and toes on my right hand and foot still refused to bloom. It didn't take a private eye to follow my trail in the December snow; my normal left shoe print was accompanied by a continuous squiggle rather than anything resembling a right shoe print.

Had I been wrong to leave the Rehab Institute in the middle of my recovery? Should I have said no to the leg brace because it made life too easy for my right foot? Or did I just need a better exercise program?

At the semester break my father called Dr. Keggi. They agreed that I should start going to the PT Department at Yale–New Haven Hospital instead of to Student Health. After exams in January, I said goodbye to the O'Malleys and began my new routine, taking a taxi across town to the hospital— where the therapists actually knew what they were doing.

Dad also found the best, if not the only, acupuncturist in southern Connecticut and arranged for a consultation. A friend with a car drove me to a white clapboard house on Long Island Sound, ten miles from campus. There, Mr. Lee, recently arrived from the Far East, put needles in my hands, my back, and my ankles. The needles didn't hurt, but they didn't help either. After three visits, Mr. Lee, a short, bald man of forty who smelled of tea and witch hazel, bowed politely and announced that he really couldn't do anything for me.

Surprisingly, this seemed to be the attitude of the doctors and therapists at the Rehab Institute when I returned at the end of my freshman year. In the Physical Therapy Department, Mrs. Walsh introduced me to a new doctor, "This is Steve. He's our miracle."

I had never thought of myself in those terms and felt uncomfortable with the designation. Of course, being a miracle was much better than the alternative, but I had no desire to be identified as an exception to the rule, an anomaly, or, worse, a medical curiosity. I realized that by getting onto the crutches, I had defied the predictions and prognoses of the experts. It was enough for Mrs. Walsh to be able to tell the doctor, "This is Steve." That was miracle enough for me.

"I've heard a lot about you," said the doctor to whom Mrs. Walsh introduced me. "So, what are your goals now?"

"To get off the crutches," I said. Could there ever have been a more obvious answer? I looked at him as if he were crazy not to know exactly what my goal was.

"No," the doctor said gravely, "I mean your career goals." And he looked at me just as Dr. Meyer had when I first insisted that I had wiggled my toe.

One of us still didn't get it.

CHAPTER 10

Although my E-Z-GO could get me from point A to point B in New Haven, I had been dependent on parents and friends for transportation at home because my right foot and leg remained too weak to operate a car's accelerator. But by the summer following my freshman year, I was determined to start driving again. While the automobile has always symbolized freedom to young American men, it truly represented independence to me. If I could drive again, I could get myself down to the RIC—where I again had the "summer job" of getting stronger—and to other places. I could go out on dates by myself.

My father, the fixer, had again done the necessary research. Just as he had found everything from the right neurosurgeon to the right rehabilitation institute, he had located a service that taught people to drive cars equipped with hand controls. But, anxious as I was to get back behind the wheel, I was not overjoyed by this particular discovery. I had been hoping to avoid hand controls; I wanted to drive like everyone else—foot to the pedal, arm free to put around that special girl. Or at least change the radio station.

During my first driving lesson, I found that I could brake with my strong left foot. Unfortunately, I could not reach the

accelerator, at least not safely, with that foot and was forced
to use the hand accelerator. "You know, there's a special device you might be interested in," my instructor told me.

I relayed the information to Dad. And so, a few weeks later,
a midnight blue Chevy Malibu with white convertible top appeared in our driveway. The new car was loaded with extras—
power windows, power door locks, air conditioning, and
quadraphonic stereo—and one extra extra: a second accelerator positioned to the left of the brake and attached by a bar to
the regular gas pedal. Stepping down on the left accelerator
with my left foot triggered the bar, which in turn depressed the
right accelerator. "We'll practice in parking lots until you get
the feel again," Dad said, handing me the keys.

After a weekend in a deserted shopping center lot, I was
ready for the open road, surprised how willing the right foot
was to let the left foot assert its supremacy. When I had to
react quickly and hit the brakes, the left foot took charge; the
right was just along for the ride. Dad and I drove south along
Sheridan Road and then took Lake Shore Drive into the city. I
did fine until we reached the S-curve at Ohio Street. A car cut
in front, and I was slow to brake. I swerved, coming far too
close to putting us in the Chicago River. Dad started for the
steering wheel, but restrained himself. By the time we got
home, I was confident.

And now I am off to a movie—*The Thomas Crown Affair*,
starring Steve McQueen and Faye Dunaway—on my own in
the car for the first time in almost two years. Mom and Dad
stand at the door just as they did when I soloed for the first
time at sixteen. I've got a date with Missy Gorman, an old
friend who happens to have been one of the best-looking girls
in our high school class. She's smart (she's a student at Bryn

Mawr), but daffy; she's seeing a psychiatrist four times a week and talks a lot about Sylvia Plath's suicide. We've gone out twice since I've been home from school. Missy says I make her feel more stable, and she feels comfortable baring her problems to me.

That's all she's baring. Before we went out, she informed me that she has a boyfriend out West with whom she's sleeping, and that ours would be, to use her words, "a basically platonic relationship."

I can live with that. With my body the way it is, it's much less important that I *be* with a girl than *be seen* with one. Particularly, one as pretty as Missy. How I'm perceived in public is somehow more important than what goes on in private. If a pretty girl wants to be with me despite the crutches, then the crutches must not matter.

Alone in the car on the way to Missy's, I feel liberated. I race another car off the stoplight and win. Suddenly, the accident doesn't matter. I'm as fast as anybody else. At the next light, a girl and I exchange glances. I'm also as desirable as anyone else.

With Missy now next to me, I draw envious stares from some guys who are just cruising. In the car, I'm as lucky as anyone else, too.

When we get to the movie theater, Missy gets out, but I just sit behind the wheel. Content. Strong.

"Do you need help?" she asks.

"No."

On the way in, she tells me she is "superdepressed" because her therapist is going out of town for a week. I repress the urge to project my thoughts to her and say that I have never been to a therapist or psychologist, don't believe in them, think they're a sign of weakness, that I believe the answer to problems emotional as well as physical must come from within. I call this philosophy the "Fiffer Code." The Code catalogs numerous other activities which I deem signs of weakness: drinking coffee, smoking cigarettes, dope, aspirin for headaches, taking Novocain for teeth-cleaning. I won't allow myself any of these foibles and count myself better than those who need artificial stimulants, lack self-restraint, can't tolerate pain, quit. To survive my accident, I need to avoid any appearance of weakness and to find any means for feeling superior to others. I could never date anyone who fell short of the Code—unless, of course, she is pretty. Beauty completely mitigates my intolerance.

Missy wants to go home after the movie so she can write something in the journal she keeps for her therapist before she forgets it. She also records her dreams. "Do you dream a lot?" she asks me as we near her house.

"A fair amount."

"When you do, are you on crutches or do you walk like you used to?"

"Mostly I walk like before."

"Sometimes I wish I could live in my dreams," Missy says wistfully. "You must, too."

"I don't really think about that," I say honestly. I don't want to think about it, or I'll probably end up on some psychiatrist's couch like Missy has.

It is only eleven when I drop her off. I start home, but something makes me direct the car toward Chicago. At the first stoplight, I look to the back seat to make sure my crutches are on the floor, invisible to the outsider. Let those on the road and the street who peer in see only my upper half. I'm like a mermaid. Appealing? Perhaps. Functional? Not so much.

THREE QUARTERS, TWO DIMES, AND A NICKEL   135

As I cross from Evanston into the city, I find myself at another light. My Malibu idles next to a car driven by an attractive older woman. I catch the woman's eye and smile as I imagine a successful playboy would. It is an inviting smile, subtle, but knowing. And all bluff. The woman sees me, and turns away quickly. When the light changes, she waits for me to pull out first.

I have forgotten. This is Chicago. There are perverts on the street, hustling and hassling women. That's not what I am, not what I want to do.

I'm not looking for a pickup. I'm looking for something more elusive, less describable. Not sex and the potential for awkwardness or even failure, but the recognition by some anonymous being that sex with me would be desirable, potentially easy and wonderful. The Immaculate Conception.

I pass by a twenty-four-hour grocery. A small, plain woman of about thirty walks out, carrying a shopping bag. I slow down. We make eye contact. I look at her hand. No wedding ring. I smile. She seems wary, but smiles back and continues walking. I intentionally miss the light at the corner she is approaching. She pauses to rest. I smile again.

"Is that bag as heavy as it looks?" I ask out the window. She nods shyly. "I could give you a ride home," I say. My heart is racing.

"Okay," she says.

She climbs in. I am afraid to make eye contact with her. "Just tell me where you want to go," I say. My throat feels very dry.

She directs me, then asks, "Do you live around here?"

I look straight ahead. "No, ma'am."

"Call me Sandy."

My palms are sweating.

Sandy continues. "What's a nice young man like you doing down here tonight?"

"I was at a movie. I dropped my date off early and I felt restless."

"I don't usually take rides, but you look safe." She looks me over. "You're Jewish, aren't you?"

I nod.

"You know my brother is president of a big congregation in Evanston."

Isn't this romantic.

We reach her apartment building. My head is throbbing. I don't know what to do or say. She gets out. "Thanks a lot," she says. Is it my imagination, or does she pause and wait for me to act? I'm silent. She heads down her walkway.

I'm out of my body, but I hear myself call, "Wait." I have to know.

Sandy comes back toward the car.

"Listen," I say, "I'm not trying to be creepy or anything, but I enjoyed meeting you. Would you like to get together sometime, like for a cup of coffee or something."

Sandy smiles. "Why not? Let me write my number down for you."

After I pull away, I crumple the paper she wrote on and drop it out the window.

I get to the coffee shop early, find a booth, and hide my crutches. Sandy is right on time. She's had her hair done and she wears a cocktail dress. She takes my hand. "Let's get out of here and go back to my place," she says without sitting down.

I rise easily, confidently, and follow her, my crutches left behind.

"You're very attractive," she says, directing me to sit on the stuffed couch in her small living room. She kisses me on the forehead and moves toward the bedroom. "Just give me a minute to change," she smiles, then closes the door behind her.

I pick up a magazine from the coffee table. I laugh. It is the bulletin from her brother's temple. I stand up and rub my crotch. "Get ready, junior."

"Okay, Steve," I hear from the bedroom. "You can come in."

I move to the door with grace and speed. Missy Gorman, not Sandy, sits naked on the bed, her long brown hair tumbling down her smooth tan shoulders, her perfect body waiting for mine.

"I don't have any problems in my dreams," says Missy, putting her journal on the nightstand. "Why don't you join me?"

But as I start for the bed my legs give out. I fall to the floor, and before Missy can reach me I have reached myself. Another me is pulling me back out the door. I fight, but I am no match for myself. "Why can't I stay?" I cry. "Why can't I stay?"

I pull the Malibu into my parents' driveway before I can answer myself.

CHAPTER 11

The Air France agent tells us that we have ten minutes to get to the opposite end of the Miami airport, where a plane is readying for departure to the Caribbean island of Martinique. My parents, Jim and Tommy, and my Aunt Ruth and cousin Sue run ahead to the gate. If we miss this flight, as we missed the previous one, we will have to wait three more hours for another. Because of an unexpected late March blizzard that marooned us at O'Hare overnight, we have already lost a day of this spring vacation.

My Uncle Bud, assigned to accompany me to the gate, motions to an empty wheelchair. "Get in," he orders.

"No," I say. I start walking.

Bud grabs the wheelchair and follows. "What is wrong with you?"

"I don't like wheelchairs." I plod forward, aware that I am licking my lips each time I take a step. Like the swishing of a racehorse's tail near the finish line, this tic is a sure sign that I am faltering. My body needs salt. My body needs rest.

After a sleepless night at O'Hare, we have spent all morning playing dot to dot with airplanes—Chicago to Cincinnati, where we hurried to catch a plane to Atlanta, where we hurried to catch a plane to Orlando, where we hurried to catch a plane to Miami, where we have already missed one flight and are in danger (thanks to me) of missing a second. The treks through five airports, the trips up and down airplane stairways, have taken their toll. I can barely move my crutches.

"We only have five minutes," Bud says. "I don't understand this."

How can I explain? I would love to sit down and let my uncle push me, but I have resolved never to ride in a wheelchair again. Under ideal conditions it is difficult to explain the importance of this vow—my need to avoid any signs that indicate I'm not independent. When seven other people are rushing for an airplane, it is impossible to make them understand.

"Can't," I pant.

A few steps later the argument is academic. My legs lock. Bud slips the wheelchair under me the way a short-order cook would slip a spatula under a fried egg, and we're off. We reach the tarmac just as the plane's stairway is about to be removed. I'm rested enough to make the climb; no other family member or passenger needs to know I cheated.

Dad already has a Bloody Mary in hand. "I have no idea how accessible this boat will be," he tells me again as we take off. "If you had just given me more notice, I could have planned."

Several weeks earlier, I had declined his invitation to take additional time after my sophomore-year spring break and join everyone on a trip to the Windward Islands. Then, forty-eight hours before their scheduled departure for Martinique and mine for New Haven, I had changed my mind and insisted on coming.

"It will be okay," I say.

Dad orders a second Bloody Mary. This has been a difficult year for him. In late February, he spent a day with me in New

Haven following a business trip to New York. We ate dinner in the college, then he took a seat on the back of the E-Z-GO, and we drove through the icy streets of the city to a movie house showing three spaghetti westerns starring his favorite actor, Clint Eastwood.

Dad seemed unusually tired during the visit. He had put on weight and had started smoking cigarettes again instead of cigars. Sadness had invaded his eyes. Before he left New Haven, he explained that one of his law partners, Dino D'Angelo, had suffered a nervous breakdown and was now on a psychiatric ward at Michael Reese Hospital. Dino had been one of his best friends since law school. They had merged firms in 1964, after each of their partners had been elected judge. I had not seen my father so beaten since the Rossis' Christmas visit in the hospital. He looked so much older than forty-three.

Over spring break, Mom had begged me to be on my best behavior because Dad was emotionally devastated by Dino's illness and physically exhausted by his partner's absence from the office. I tried my hardest. The break had been so pleasant that I had decided to prolong it by going on the trip.

Dad and Uncle Bud have chartered a ninety-foot motor yacht, the *LaMarie*. By the time I've negotiated a short wooden plank that runs from the dock to the boat's entrance, Mom has surfaced from the below-deck living quarters. "You can't go down there," she says solemnly. "It's too dangerous. You'll fall."

"Nonsense."

The steep iron steps of the winding stairway narrow as I descend. It takes me fifteen minutes to reach the bottom, longer to struggle back up. "See," I say.

Mom doesn't see. "There are seven other people on this trip. We are not going to spend all our time watching what you can prove."

"The ship is not even moving now," says the rheumy-eyed captain, diplomatic, but clearly dismayed at the special case on board.

I will have to sleep in the stark white auxiliary dining room on the main deck. The only toilet is downstairs. Before we depart, Mom goes into town to buy a bedpan and urinal.

Despite calm seas and the yacht's stabilizers, I cannot rise from a seat or walk more than a few steps once we are moving. I drop anchor in a chair for the day. Even when the ship isn't moving, I need help getting from room to room because there are high steps in all doorways to prevent flooding from the seas. I must lean on Jim or Dad or Bud to climb over these.

Whenever we reach a port, the crew takes out a flimsy wood-plank stairway with a rope "handrail" for the passengers to go ashore. I can't go up or down this—even with the help of Kurt, the tall, blond first mate who is built like a linebacker. My trips from ship to shore are accomplished via the bos'n's chair—a swinglike apparatus normally used by crew members to work on the side of the yacht. As Kurt pushes me above the water to nervously waiting hands on the dock, I sit on the narrow green seat clenching the ropes like five-year-old Tommy does on the big kids' swing at school.

On land or sea, each step I take—or don't take—reminds me of my insufficiencies. It has been almost two and a half years since the accident, and I have gradually adjusted to maneuvering around Yale and home. But this trip leaves no leeway for gradual adjustment.

Movement is impossible, so, forgetting Mom's pleas to make life easy for Dad, I become impossible. Mom hacks after smoking a cigarette. "That is so disgusting," I say. "I can't imagine what your lungs look like." Dad eats a second helping of key lime pie. "You've had an extra dessert with every dinner this week," I tell him. "Are you a candidate for a heart attack or what?"

What would happen to me if something happened to them? After a week of hell, we fly to New York's Kennedy Airport. The family waits for its flight back to Chicago; I wait for the bus back to New Haven. All the chairs in the lounge are occupied, so I sit on my suitcase.

My mother approaches. She has not spoken to me for two days. "I think you should seriously consider getting an apartment of your own this summer," she says. "Because if you behave anything like the way you did on this trip, you are not going to live in my house." She turns away before I can respond.

I feel the suitcase start to collapse. I try to right myself, but can't. I crumple with the luggage to the floor, embarrassed but unhurt. No one from the family moves to help. A porter picks me up.

.　　.　　.

I see myself slumped against the gray wall in Kennedy Airport, body shaped like a question mark, waiting for the bus back to New Haven. There is a helplessness etched in my face at this moment, a helplessness that has been growing in recent weeks. It's not the same feeling I had right after the accident when I couldn't control my body. It is a helplessness of spirit. For the first time, I am beginning to doubt. Doubt that this will be over soon. Dare I say it, *ever*. The progress has slowed so much. My work during the past summer at the Rehab Institute and this school year with the therapists at Yale–New Haven don't seem to have gotten me anywhere.

"Plateaus are to be expected," the doctors at RIC had said on the eve of my return to New Haven for my second year. Then they again reminded me how miraculous my recovery had been. "You're a walking quadriplegic," they said. "There aren't too many of those around. You should count your blessings." Instead, I was counting the number of days it had been since I woke up to find something new wiggling again. How long had it been since I was able to measure the improvement in weeks, not months?

I can't abide plateaus. I'm nineteen. The sky should be the limit, not some plateau. I should be playing hard. Working hard. I should be fucking my brains out like the rest of my friends, but I'm not. I've only had one relationship that could even be called "serious."

After I started driving again, I went to a party where I ran into Ellie Fine, a friend from junior high. We had won a dance contest together back then, but we had lost track of each other in high school. She had just completed her first year at the University of Wisconsin. She already knew that she wanted to be an occupational therapist, so we found much to talk about. She was sensitive and artistic. Her pleasant round face and terrific figure were as I remembered, but her light brown hair was considerably longer than it had been in eighth grade; an elaborate braid followed her spine all the way down to her waist. I thought she looked very sexy. We saw each other for the rest of the summer.

In November of our sophomore year, Ellie flew to New Haven for the Yale-Harvard football weekend. She arrived well after midnight, and, exhausted from her two-plane, one-bus journey, collapsed on the foldout couch in the living area of the two-room suite I now shared with Bob Bissell. I slept in the bedroom. By the next night, we knew we wanted to sleep together.

Ellie was a free spirit. She worked daily with disabled people in her occupational therapy classes and had never made me feel self-conscious about my physical shortcomings. I don't think she had any problem with my body. But I did. As we moved closer to making love, I put on the brakes. I simply wasn't sure how well I would be able to perform and feared that awkwardness would jeopardize our future relationship. We fell asleep with our arms around one another.

I never offered Ellie an explanation and she never asked for one. She seemed to sense my fears and graciously allowed me the time to work them out on my own without bringing them up for discussion. That time never came for us. We saw each other daily over Christmas break, joined Bill Solomon and his girlfriend at Second City for New Year's Eve, and then parted in the spring after she fell in love with a classmate at Wisconsin. That night in November was the closest I had come to making love. The sexual revolution may have arrived for others, but like the wounded young man in the famous American Revolutionary scene, this Fiffer is limping behind.

I have tried my hardest to get rid of that limp, have exercised religiously. The Rehab Institute, Uncle Bud's pool, Student Health, the Yale pool, Yale–New Haven Hospital. At the end of freshman year, I met Mom and Dad in Boston, where a new battery of specialists ran me through a series of tests. Before going back to New Haven for my sophomore year, I went to the clinic at Warm Springs, Georgia, where Franklin Roosevelt was treated. An atlas full of places to become an Atlas.

I have become a human laboratory experiment. They have iced me, heated me, and electroshocked me to stimulate motion. They have tried steel and aluminum, single-posted and double-barred braces to keep my right foot from dropping. I have had passive range-of-motion therapy; I have had active resistance therapy; I have tried dumbbells and isometrics, crawling and climbing. Acupuncture.

Before we left on our trip, a former neighbor stopped by. He's about eighty, short and portly and bald—a good Irish Catholic who stutter-steps three blocks to mass each morning. He's probably the only person I know I could beat in the fifty-yard dash. He hobbled into our house, drank a cup of tea with trembling hands, and said, "It's too bad you're not of my faith, Steve. There's this place in France called Lourdes."

Lourdes! Why not? *I am losing control.*

I am tired. Tired of exercising. Tired of the stares of people on the street. Tired of the leg bag that continues to dam my confidence and spontaneity. I am tired of being so defensive, so self-conscious around women, so afraid to use my body. I am tired of watching every step I take so that I won't fall on my face again. I want to look up, not down.

Most of all, I am tired of being everyone's miracle, everyone's hero, everyone's source of strength. How many times have I been told: "My problems are so small compared to what you've been through. If you can overcome yours, then I can overcome mine." Or: "Just watching you gives me the courage to keep going."

I remember reading a myth about a Spartan boy who was carrying a live wolf under his tunic. The wolf was gnawing at his stomach, so the boy tried to hurry home. But people—unaware of his predicament—kept stopping him. The wolf's gnawing became more and more painful, but the boy refused to reveal his vulnerability to those seeking his assistance. He was, after all, a Spartan. What was his reward for showing such strength? By the time he finally reached home, he had been eaten alive by the wolf.

I'm tired of carrying the wolf, being a Spartan.

I am tired, but I cannot afford to be tired. Like a fallen

mountain climber clinging to a ledge, I cannot afford to give up. I cannot let my will fail—because the major reason for success up to now is that I willed recovery. Mind over matter. I wasn't supposed to walk again. I wanted to walk again. So I did. My ignorance those early days in the hospital was indeed blissful. Now that I know the odds I face, the doctors' prognoses, it is more difficult to keep the will alive. Especially without the reinforcement of improving each day.

And so, I feel myself slipping. My weight is up, my class attendance and grades are down. I'm not drinking enough water to flush my kidneys. Personal hygiene doesn't seem as important. I've even smoked dope a few times—something I had sworn I would never do because I don't like to and can't afford to be out of control. And now this dreadful exhibition on the trip.

I am slipping. And though I keep telling myself I will never let go, I am not so sure I can hold on much longer.

I want to be whole. I want to lead a normal life.

But I am so tired.

．　　　．　　　．

One of the people that *I* looked up to was also on the airport bus to New Haven. Andy Coe had been the football captain at my high school when I was a sophomore. He had also been the captain of the Yale varsity, this his senior year. I had not known him at New Trier, but we had become friends earlier in the year when we shared a ride to Washington, D.C., and, with numerous other students, lobbied Congress to stop funding the war in Vietnam. This had been my second trip to the capital during my sophomore year. In November, I had joined 250,000 other antiwar protesters from across the country. Unable to march, I worked in a first-aid station set up in a church.

Andy, a sturdy, crew-cut six-footer with what appeared to be a permanent crease in his forehead from wearing a football helmet for the last eight years, had not made political waves while captain of the team. But as soon as the season ended, he took a leadership role in peacefully protesting the war (and began letting his sandy brown hair grow).

On December 1, everyone on campus listened breathlessly to the draft lottery. Someone set up a poster board in the Timothy Dwight Dining Hall and filled in the birth dates next to the corresponding draft lottery numbers. We had been told that numbers 1 through 125 faced a good chance of being drafted within the next year. The voice on the radio called out the numbers as calmly as if this were a macabre game of bingo. The dining hall was silent as a funeral; those dodging the bullet by receiving numbers in the 300s remained respectful of the others in the room and across the country who were not so fortunate.

Andy's number, 137, left him in limbo. The son of a minister, he had been brought up to value human life and abhor war, and so he decided to apply for conscientious objector status. If such status wasn't granted, he was prepared to go to jail. This was a bold step for any young man to take, but was particularly dramatic for Andy. As the captain of the football team at a school like Yale and an All–Ivy League linebacker, he had a bright future assured if he cared to play ball after graduation with the old-boy network that wielded tremendous influence in business, the law, and government—and which, for the most part, still supported the war. For decades, the captains of industry had eagerly employed and promoted the captains of Ivy League football teams.

I would gladly have given Andy my number in the high

200s. I didn't need it, because after some debate my draft board had finally declared me physically ineligible. Remarkably, there had actually been a debate. The board had initially sent me a 1Y student deferment, indicating that I was physically capable of serving. My father had written back to inform the board that I was on crutches due to a paralyzing injury and should be reclassified 4F. Apparently, this explanation wasn't sufficient. Dad and the board exchanged several more letters until finally, as amused as he was exasperated, Dad told the board they could have me.

On the bus ride back to school following my return from the jungles of the Windward Islands, Andy reminded me that the civil rights lawyer and political activist William Kuntsler would be at Yale later in the week to speak about the upcoming murder trial in New Haven of Black Panther Bobby Seale. We went to the speech together. While odd-looking, crew-cut men in sport coats (whom we later realized were undercover FBI agents) took pictures in the hall, Kuntsler energized the crowd by painting a picture of a government conspiracy to frame Seale, who had gained national notoriety when bound and gagged by Judge Julius Hoffman at the trial of the Chicago 7.

From this warm April day until summer break six weeks later, I put politics before school, as did most of the student body. Perhaps equally important, I put politics before me. There was no room for self-pity in my busy, meaningful, directed new life as a protester; no time to be tired. When we weren't calling for the Justice Department to investigate the trial of Bobby Seale, we were calling for the university to register its protest of the government conspiracy, to take better care of its workers, and to support Black Panther initiatives. (Young black children roamed through dormitories soliciting for local Panther breakfast programs, and the most popular T-shirt on campus featured a black panther and a Yale bulldog side by side.) Eventually, the vast majority of students went on strike for several days to protest Yale's alleged failures in the community, its unsatisfactory treatment of its own employees, and its curriculum's failure to properly address social issues.

Radical leaders from outside the university and from outside New Haven organized a May Day rally to protest everything from the treatment of Seale and the Black Panthers to the war in Vietnam. The governor of Connecticut called in the National Guard. Fearing violence, many students left the campus. Those of us who stayed received instructions on how to react if tear-gassed. We raised money for a bond pool in the event that fellow students needed to be bailed out of jail. At Timothy Dwight, I held this money. (Recognizing that I would be unable to run if the Guard used gas, bullets, or bayonets, I decided not to go to the rally. Instead, I would stay behind the college walls, easy to find if the bail money was needed.)

On the eve of the rally, National Guardsmen, many of them as young and as frightened as we were, gathered on the sidewalks outside our windows. They carried rifles that, we were told, had no ammunition. Some students went outside and stuck flowers in the soldiers' gun barrels. The Guardsmen did not react.

My roommate Bob was on the varsity crew team, which was competing out of town on May 1. He left reluctantly on April 30. I knew that in the event of trouble, he would have selflessly helped me to safety. Alone in our room that night, I slept with my shoes on—just in case I needed to make a fast exit.

The May Day rally in New Haven proved relatively peaceful. We were lucky. Three days later, the Ohio National Guard opened fire on Kent State students protesting the renewed bombing of Cambodia. Four died.

Although I had grown less trusting and respectful of government in the days leading up to Kent State, I prided myself on being objective, balanced, and nonhypocritical in evaluating the issues and determining a course of action (at least for a nineteen-year-old). I found it strange, for example, that many of my fellow students watching the news each night in the TD television room would cheer whenever Walter Cronkite announced that the stock market was down. While the market may have been a symbol of the wicked military-industrial complex, most of us were getting our B.A.'s thanks to our parents' wise investments in IBM, GM, and the like. Kent State, however, pushed me over the edge. It was Us against Them now as far as I was concerned.

Until I stopped going to classes (along with the vast majority of others at Yale), my father had not quarreled about my conduct. As an undergraduate at the University of Chicago in the mid-1940s, he had published a newspaper so radical that he had been threatened with expulsion. As a young lawyer, he had helped shape the agenda for progressive Democratic state legislators. While he was a mainstream Democrat now, he did oppose the war—although it had taken him longer to see the light than I liked; for years he had insisted that while the war appeared to be without merit, the government must know more than it was letting on.

We had discussed my protests against the upcoming Bobby Seale murder trial. My father, who knew Julius Hoffman, had been so incensed by the judge's behavior at the Chicago 7 trial that he would not even speak to him when their paths crossed in the Federal Building or the Standard Club, where each often ate lunch. But Dad believed in our legal system and insisted that Seale could get a fair trial in New Haven. When I explained that my protest was aimed at forcing the national spotlight on the courtroom to insure that fair trial, Dad didn't agree with my opinion, but he respected it.

He considered supporting the Black Panthers and striking against Yale, however, completely different. I still have the letter he wrote me. "Some random thoughts," he began. Ten numbered paragraphs followed:

1. Do not confuse the process of feeling about a problem with the process of thinking about a problem. They are separate and distinct.

2. The fact that one has nothing personal to gain from an action is no guarantee that the action is either intelligent or worthwhile. Much stupidity has been carried on in the name of altruism. Most of the real horrors of history have been perpetrated in the name of pure goodness, e.g., the Inquisition, the Salem witch burnings, the Nazi holocaust, even Viet Nam.

3. Dissent is the expression of a contrary opinion. It contemplates the transmission of ideas and words, not rocks, bricks, bombs, or other dangerous missiles.

4. The concept of you striking against a university to whom we pay $3,600 for the privilege of attending classes strikes me as more than slightly Orwellian—perhaps less *is* more.

5. I must assume that by now the administration of the university is aware of the views of the student body with respect to day care and other employee benefits and for reasons deemed appropriate has not adopted the student

program. I find it difficult to understand why, especially in a university dedicated to reason, the resolution of a problem such as this should be determined by superior force.

6. That society may have perpetrated injustice upon the Black Panthers makes me wish to correct the injustice, as I would wish to correct injustice done to any man.

7. That society has perpetrated injustices upon the Black Panthers does not lend one iota of validity to their programs, their rhetoric, or their activities generally. These must be viewed on their merits.

8. I regard the Panthers as dangerous and counterproductive to the interests of those they purport to serve. They are dangerous because they act upon the principle that the ends justifies the means. I do not believe in this principle because I believe, along with John Dewey, the ends are continually redefined in terms of the means employed to achieve them. . . . I do not wish to live in a society where every man who feels aggrieved, whether rightly or wrongly, is free to take his gun, his bomb, his mob, or any other "weapon" and in his own way threaten, disturb, or harm my life or rights. . . . It is because of the Panthers, RAM, and SDS, that we must give "thanks" for the prospect of yet another four years of Ronald Reagan in California and to the disturbingly widespread acceptance of the words of Spiro T. Agnew.

9. I hope that your participation in the "passion of your time" is as instructive as you think it will be. I would ask, however, that you be alert to notice when you have learned from it all that you can reasonably expect to

learn. At that point (consistent with your social responsibilities) the resumption of class attendance would seem to be the most promising way to further your education.

10. I am proud of your sensitivity to injustice, pleased with your ability to respond to problems with thought as well as emotion, unhappy that you will miss some excellent classes, envious of the exhilaration of an all-consuming cause (I've known it), slightly concerned for your physical well-being, and confident that you will survive your days on the barricades as I survived mine.

Much love,

Dad

This letter moves me to tears each time I read it. My father typed this at home on a Sunday evening—most likely after I had called to update him on events at school. I picture him in the study at his old Royal typewriter, pecking away, then pausing to make sure that the tone and words were clear—that he temper his own philosophy and passion with his respect for the right of his oldest son to grow up and even make mistakes. I think that even a stranger can see in this letter that this was a man who, unlike so many others, would have had the courage to let that son go so far way to college so soon after a devastating accident, to give that son as much independence as possible.

With almost thirty years' hindsight, I agree with much of what Dad said. The strike, I now believe, was ill advised. Still, I don't regret my actions or the actions of my fellow students in 1970; our hearts were in the right place.

Some fifteen years later, my brother Tom, then a sophomore at Yale, telephoned me from school. "We just had our first sit-in," he said excitedly.

Vietnam was over. The Panthers were long gone. I tried to figure out the issue that had so engaged Tom. I had read that the university was thinking about tearing down a shanty that students had built on campus to protest Yale's investments in South Africa. I asked Tom if he'd been protesting against apartheid.

"No," he said. "We're protesting cutbacks in library hours." He explained that he and his friends had refused to leave the library at closing time. A campus policeman had to push them out. The times they were a-changin'.

PART THREE

Dick Woit may be the world's top physical fitness expert. He is certainly one of the most controversial leaders of them. Dick, you see, is the man everybody loves to hate. Gale Sayers in his book, *I Am Third,* calls Woit "Hitler." Others call him worse. Or just "The Meanest Man in the World." And why not? He demeans All Pro athletes. He verbally abuses doctors and lawyers and captains of industry—men who are at the tops in their professions. And he slugs cripples.

Chicago Tribune, 2/28/71

CHAPTER 12

The room was only twenty-five feet by thirty. Wooden benches, their orange paint peeling, ringed aging rubber wrestling mats cluttered with barbells badly in need of soldering. The yellow brick walls were sweating as much as the occupants.

I had almost forgotten the smell, that singularly vital scent of men pushing their bodies to the limit. It conjured memories of the gyms in which I once played. There existed a kind of magic between those rooms, too, and their inhabitants. The gyms taking on the smell of the athletes (a smell which no amount of airing could destroy) and the athletes adopting the personality of the room—no-nonsense functional.

Two summers at the Rehabilitation Institute and I had never picked up that smell. The place did wonders for me—at least that first year. But the environment was so clinical, white, sterile.

The cluster of men in the corner hadn't noticed me standing in the doorway. I recognized some of them as members of the Chicago Bears. They surrounded a man bench-pressing a huge amount of weight. I didn't recognize the lifter, who according to the count of a small red-haired man had pressed his barbell 130 times.

When the count reached 150, the lifter's arms began to shake, the interval between presses became longer, and a look of anguish, up to now only transient, took permanent residence. Everyone was silent except for the counter. "C'mon you motherfucker," he bellowed. "You ain't worth shit if you can't do two hundred."

When the lifter rested the weight on his chest at 175, the counter pulled his hair and barked, "Keep going you sheeny bastard." Transfused by the tirade, the man pumped the weight another 25 times. The room erupted in applause.

"Not bad, Weisman," said the counter. "If you had two lungs you could probably do four hundred."

The men swaggered confidently past me out of the exercise room. Weisman remained on the bench, smiling and gasping.

The redheaded counter took the weight, which looked bigger than he was, and easily carried it to an iron rack near the doorway. I stepped forward.

"What do you want, Crip?" the man asked me.

"I'm here to see Mr. Woit."

"You're looking at him. I'm Dick Woit."

I introduced myself and reminded him that I had spoken with him on the phone the previous day. I hoped my voice did not show my surprise. The newspaper article waiting on my pillow when I returned home after my sophomore year had profiled a hard-nosed former pro football player who now conditioned athletes, businessmen, and a handful of the infirm at the Lawson YMCA on Chicago's Near North Side. Dick Woit was best known for having trained Bears star Gale Sayers after the halfback had suffered what many thought would be a career-ending knee injury. Instead, after an off-season with Woit, Sayers had returned to lead the National Football League in rushing.

Woit's harsh demeanor—no one had ever called me "Crip"— fit the profile, but he seemed too tiny to be a retired Detroit Lions running back. He couldn't be more than five feet seven inches tall, couldn't weigh more than 130 pounds. I knew that size wasn't everything. I'd seen wrestlers and weight lifters with those vital statistics whose bulging necks and arms suggested unlimited strength and invincibility. But Woit was not only small, he was gaunt. His pale cheeks looked like they'd been sunk with ballast. I couldn't tell how old he was. Perhaps forty.

"Fiffer? Oh yeah. Jesus, Weisman, will you look at the belly on this son of a bitch." Weisman was still on the bench trying to fill his lungs, or lung. "Kid," Woit said to me, "you got a good twenty pounds to lose. How can you look at yourself in the mirror?" He motioned to my crutches. "Do you really need those things?"

I nodded. I wasn't more than ten pounds overweight, and of course I needed the crutches. I debated whether to give my medical history to this man with the obvious Napoleon complex. No. One of the problems had been that the therapists at Rehab kept congratulating me on how far I'd come. I needed someone to tell me how far I still had to go.

"Can you do a sit-up?"

"I think so."

"Shit, Crip, get down on the floor and try."

I rested my crutches against the wall, sat on a nearby bench, lowered myself to the hardwood floor, and then edged to an adjacent mat.

"Hold it. You don't need the mat. Do it on the floor."

Movements which were once accomplished automatically now required rumination. I had only done sit-ups on a tilted board at Rehab. Gravity had been an ally.

I considered the best approach to doing a real sit-up. Extending my arms behind my head, I tightened my stomach and then jerked-threw all my weight forward. Surprise! I got all the way up. Did Little Napoleon possess some magic that allowed the injured and ill to do the impossible?

I remained in the up position, smiling.

"Again."

Okay. To achieve even greater thrust, I threw my arms back as I returned to the starting position. This provided additional momentum for the next attempt. Unfortunately, it also propelled my head into the floor.

I managed three more full sit-ups, banging my head each time. On my next try, I only got halfway up, but there was no order to stop. Indeed, there was no order to stop for another two minutes. One hundred twenty seconds punctuated by heavy breathing and frequent cracks of the skull against the floor. When Woit finally instructed me to rest, my stomach felt like Jell-O, my head like a suitable whipped-cream topping. I was woozy, but even if I hadn't been, I still couldn't have read his face.

"Which leg is stronger?"

"The left. I still have a short brace on the right."

"Can you bend the left one while you're on your back?"

"Sure." I pulled it halfway up to my chest.

"How about the right?"

"I don't know." I tried, casually at first. Nothing. I tried again, this time closing my eyes, grimacing, tightening my fists and every other muscle that worked. Still nothing. "I can make it play dead if that's any help," I smiled. I still used the joke.

Woit didn't laugh. He bent down and squeezed my calf. "Christ, there's no fucking tone here. How long since you were hurt?"

"About two and a half years."

"What the hell have you been doing since then? Picking your nose?"

Getting therapy, swimming, going to a college that would never take you, I thought to myself. But strangely, I was not offended by the insults. The attitude of my doctors and therapists was more disturbing. They still pointed to me as the walking miracle man.

Woit hardly seemed ready to anoint me a "miracle." He made me yank a pulley attached to the wall, then lifted me up to the bench and handed me a 25-pound barbell. "Curl this," he snapped. I hadn't used a barbell since I was hurt and could only bring this light weight three-quarters of the way from my waist to my chin. "Pathetic. Stand up."

One of the men from the earlier class had returned to the room. Six feet tall, 185 pounds, all muscle and Afro, he looked familiar. "Hey, Gordon," said Woit (I realized he was talking to Dick Gordon, the Bears' wide receiver), "c'mere and catch this cripple if he starts to fall."

Gordon dutifully joined us. Woit noticed my excitement. "All right, don't pee in your pants." He pushed my back against the wall and instructed me to keep my butt against the surface and lower myself until I was on my tiptoes. He ordered Gordon to catch me on command.

Electriclike shock rifled through my legs as I struggled to avoid collapsing into the arms of the football player. My hamstrings squealed. Five seconds, ten, fifteen, and then all strength drained, I crumbled. "Catch him," yelled Woit. And the sure-handed wide receiver made the grab shortly before my head was reintroduced to the floor.

"Seventeen seconds," Woit shook his head. "Tomorrow you don't get someone to catch you until you hit twenty."

"Okay," I panted.

Woit handed me my crutches.

"Your dad got a lotta money?"

I wasn't sure what to say. "We're comfortable."

"What is he a doctor? Lawyer?"

"Lawyer."

"Well, his money ain't gonna do you any good here. You're on your own, pal."

"I know that," I said. If Woit thought that was going to scare me, he was wrong. I liked the idea of having to succeed or fail here entirely on my own, was glad my father's influence and affluence would be nonfactors. The time for using clout had passed. This was my test and mine alone.

As I was leaving, I heard Woit tell Gordon, "He seems to have balls. We'll see if he really wants it."

I smiled. My head still throbbed. My legs still ached. But all I could think of was that I'd seen half a dozen of my heroes, that one of the stars of the Chicago Bears had helped me with an exercise, and that a foul-mouthed, anorexic midget was somehow going to push me further than I'd ever been pushed.

.   .   .

During the summer of 1970, I would not have enlisted in the United States Armed Forces even if I had been physically qualified to do so. I did not hate my country as some of my classmates did, but I did not support the war in Vietnam. Nor would I have joined a cult. Barely able to control my bladder and bowels, I was not about to turn my mind over to some bald, blind, or bearded guru. Yet as the summer progressed, I realized I had turned my mind and my body over to a man part maharishi, part Marine.

Friends who came to the YMCA with me to gawk at their football heroes left amazed that I allowed Dick Woit to call me "Crip" or "Sheeny." Thankfully, my mother and father never ventured to the gym. Just as parents don't like to imagine their children having sex, I think they didn't want to know the details of what was happening in the gym. They remained cool and neutral—the Switzerland of parents—even when my right arm suddenly swelled to twice its normal size.

"Cellulitis," the doctor said. He guessed that the infection was the result of germs entering the cuts on my elbows—cuts created by dragging myself across Woit's floor and mats. Moving the arm would exacerbate the situation. I was to stay away from the gym for two weeks.

The timing couldn't have been worse. My recent progress had been almost as dramatic as it had been in the early months after the accident. In just fifteen half-hour sessions with Dick, I had increased the amount of weight I could curl from twenty-five to thirty-five pounds; I could tolerate an additional five pounds on the pulley; I could last a full ten seconds longer against the wall before collapsing; and could now manage eight full sit-ups. I had lost seven pounds; my stomach was beginning to show some tone; and my biceps were noticeably larger. I still couldn't bend my right leg, but Dick said that that would come if I wanted it badly enough, and I, of course, believed him. I was now also doing modified push-ups, and Dick had promised that if I continued to improve, I could do a modified workout alongside the jocks in the normal class. More important, the helplessness I had begun to experience, the tiredness, the feeling of slipping had all disappeared.

Dick had indicated more than once that the only excuse for missing a workout was death. ("Your own, not a relative's.") I didn't want to tell him in person that a mere infection would keep me away. I phoned when I knew he would be in one of the six classes he led each day and left my message. That night I told my parents I had to go back to the gym the next afternoon; my fear of alienating Dick and halting the momentum of recovery was more frightening than the prospect of further infection. They agreed that if I kept my arm covered and promised not to use it—worked only on my legs—I could return.

Arriving early, I sat on the bench and began to lower myself to the floor. The kick to my back that sent me face first into the mat caught me by surprise. "You crippledkikemother-fucker, if you ever miss another day, don't bother to come back." I knew the voice.

Dick was momentarily apologetic when I showed him the infection and told him I had defied doctor's orders to come. He created a makeshift cushion for the elbow and designed a workout that avoided undue movement of the arm. But the warmth was short-lived. "Don't get the impression that I'm going to baby you just because of a little infection. Next week it's back to the routine. Shit, Crip, you can't do anything with your arms, how 'bout bending your fucking leg today."

Lying flat on the floor, I tried bending the rigid right leg up toward my chest. Nothing.

"Again."

I felt a twitch, but there was no movement.

Dick somehow perceived something was happening.

"That's it. Now bend it."

I held my breath, tightened my stomach, and pulled. And the right leg, dormant for so long, bent. Perhaps only two or three inches, but it bent. Beaming, I relaxed and looked up at Dick for approval.

Booming, he shook me from my reverie. "Higher, Crip!"

"Higher? Dick, this is the first time I've bent it in two and a half years."

"I said 'higher.'"

"But, Dick—"

"Dammit, Crip." Dick kicked my weak right leg with his strong left one. Forcefully.

And before I could scream, I pulled the leg up another four inches.

.   .   .

Dick lived with his parents in a Polish neighborhood on Chicago's Northwest Side. Every Wednesday, he would lend his car to his mother. Among Woit's Warriors—the name of his cult/drill unit—it was considered a great honor if "Coach" asked you to pick him up on a Wednesday morning or drive him home that afternoon. The day after I bent my right leg, he so honored me.

I had a real summer job besides working out at the Y. When I had returned from school, Dr. Betts had called. RIC had a grant from the U.S. Department of Health, Education, and Welfare to assemble a resource library on the architectural barriers confronting the disabled. Was I interested in making $1,000, the doctor asked? I knew the barriers firsthand, faced them every day. Now I had a chance to do something to get rid of them—and get paid in the process. The Y was less than a mile from the institute. I had taken the job with the understanding that I could extend my lunch hour to work out with Dick.

After Dick asked for a ride home, I arranged to leave work early and met him at the Y at four o'clock. He was standing in front, looking at his watch when I pulled up in the Malibu. I had never seen him outside his gym kingdom before. He was still wearing his trademark maroon sweats. In the real world, walking across the sidewalk to my car among real people, he suddenly looked mortal, insignificant, *tiny*. A middle-aged woman in a hurry almost knocked him over, and he didn't say a word.

Once in my car, Dick seemed to grow, to regain stature. I should have anticipated that my messy front seat would bother him. "You can tell a lot about a person by the way he takes care of his car," he said, picking up a hot-dog wrapper and some loose change from the passenger side.

I headed west on Chicago Avenue.

"This is a nice car. You should take better care of it. I clean my car every night. Wax it every Sunday after church. Takes me three hours."

Suddenly, a white Datsun swerved in front of us.

"Look out," Dick screamed.

I hit the brakes, and we slammed to a halt inches behind the offender.

"I'll bet it was a goddamn Jap," Dick said. "They think because they can make cars they don't have to know how to drive them."

I started up again.

"So, Crip, you got a bush?"

"A bush?" I had no idea what he was talking about.

"A bush. Girl. Jesus, Crip, where have you been?"

"I just never heard the expression. A girl?" Since getting home, I had gone out a few times with one of my high school classmates who now went to Smith. I guess she qualified. "I'm dating someone, but it's nothing serious," I said.

"Well, be careful. I spend half my time listening to guys complaining about their bushes."

All I could think of was my dad lamenting that the forsythia wasn't coming in like it should this summer.

Dick opened my glove compartment and began looking through it. "Know what I do when I get home?" he said.

I shook my head.

"Well, first I go to mass with my mother. I do that every night. Then I'm on the phone calling all the guys who missed today. Half will tell me it's bush trouble. Like Miller, the lawyer in the one o'clock. He said he'd be in. Wasn't. What good is a man if he don't keep his word. Anyway, he'll tell me his wife is causing trouble, and I'll say, 'What do you expect when you try to run around with some bush on the sly.' I mean, his wife is no bargain, but let him work his fucking rocks off in the gym. You know?"

I nodded.

"Jesus, you're quiet. I've never heard of a quiet Jew. If it weren't for your nose, I wouldn't even know you're Jewish."

I considered making a U-turn and heading for the nearest office of the Anti-Defamation League.

Dick shook his fist at a driver who was moving too slowly in front of us. "Give that jerk the horn, Crip."

Reluctantly I honked.

"So as I was saying, watch the bush. I never married—"
Quelle surprise!
"—Had plenty of bush though, 'til I wised up. Yeah, plenty

of bush in those days, but then after I got hurt and started doing this—" He finally shut the glove compartment. "—Total abstinence. No way I could screw and do six workouts a day. Certainly no way I could be married with my schedule. It's better anyway. Like I say, most bush are trouble." Remarkably, he paused, looked contemplative. "Course, sometimes I think I wouldn't mind having a kid."

I sensed an intimacy developing beneath all this rambling and wasn't sure how to handle it. After an uncomfortable silence, I said, "I think I'd like to have kids someday."

Dick was looking out the window. "It's the next exit," he said.

A few blocks from the highway, he told me to stop. "I'll be just a minute," he said, and he ran into a flower shop. "For my mother," he explained when he came back.

He looked at the clock on my dashboard. "Shit. Running late. We'll barely make mass. I'd have to miss dinner, if I ate it."

I had heard rumors about this. "So it's true that you don't eat?"

He shook his head. "Locker room scuttlebutt. I eat. Half a pint of Cool Whip when I get up, the other half before I go to bed."

"But that's all?"

"That's all. Food's like sex. You can't have it and do as many workouts as I do. But I do love Cool Whip. It's my only vice. I'm getting a hard-on just thinking about it."

"Is that all you ate when you played football?"

"What are you, a lawyer?"

"Not yet," I said.

"They didn't even have Cool Whip when I played football.

You think I looked like this when I played. I weighed one seventy. My thighs were as big as that tree trunk over there, and I could bench more than Weisman. I ate anything I wanted in those days, including bush."

We pulled up to a red brick bungalow with a green awning in a neighborhood full of red brick bungalows with green awnings.

"Now keep this car clean, huh, Crip," Dick said as he climbed out. "It's gonna be a long night. Calling the guys." He shut the car door. "I don't know what you all would do without me," he said. And then he sprinted toward the house.

I certainly didn't know what I'd do without him. As determined as I had been to get myself better, I had simply run out of energy to motivate myself. My father had found Dick Woit at the perfect time. I was willing to do anything he told me. I had given him more than my mind and body. I had also turned over my soul to him in this Faustian bargain to regain my legs.

CHAPTER 13

When I started with Dick Woit, the health and fitness boom that would consume and in some ways define America was still several years away. There were hardly any health clubs. Few sportswear or sports equipment companies could be found pitching their products on television; and even fewer could be found among the Fortune 500. While some men and women were beginning to get their exercise by running in addition to playing recreational sports, only a handful "worked out." Stationary bikes were common, but there was no such thing as a Solo Flex or StairMaster, or heaven forbid, Thighmaster.

Thus, the Archie Bunker–like Dick Woit, who by today's standards might seem like a throwback to an age we would all like to forget, was in fact on the cutting edge in his chosen field, having designed forty-five punishing minutes of nonstop aerobic and anaerobic exercise featuring sit-ups, push-ups, free weights, and wind sprints. Like those in the early seventies attempting to expand their minds in new ways, Woit's Warriors sought to perfect their bodies. We were in a sense the Merry Pranksters of our day, with Dick Woit our Ken Kesey. Even the Bears who came to the gym were ahead of their time. Most professional athletes let their bodies rest during the off season, using training camp or the exhibition season to get in shape.

My motivation and the motivation of the pros and the handful of other nonathletes who came to rehabilitate bad knees or weak hearts was obvious (there were no others with spinal cord injuries). But what brought the apparently healthy lawyers, accountants, roofers, and those in almost every other profession to the gym? In part, narcissism. From their locker room banter and preening, it was apparent that most of the Warriors were going through what I had heard described as midlife crises. They talked about their new Corvettes and XKEs and the girlfriends half their age. Most remained married, but as Jerry, a plumbing contractor, put it, "For me, marriage is a base of operations." To keep their young mistresses, Jerry and the other Warriors needed to be flashy and fit.

At a Warrior party shortly after I started with Dick, I saw these men outside the gym for the first time. Almost all wore tight pants and fancy silk shirts open at the collar to reveal gold chains. Most also wore their girlfriends on their arms. Under ordinary circumstances, I could never have respected men my father's age who dressed this way, or who consorted with girls my age. Yet because of the way they conducted themselves in the world's most difficult workout, I couldn't help but respect the Warriors.

I keep using that term, Warriors. Most of Dick's followers were self-made men (many of them Jewish) who had had no time and probably no skill to participate in sports when younger. Now, for the first time they were on a team. It was this desire to be part of a team, the Warriors (plural), as much as it was to be a warrior (singular) that brought many to the gym. I could find something similar to sports in almost everything I did. But I knew I was rationalizing. Only when Dick invited, rather *ordered,* me to begin doing a modified workout alongside the regulars did I really feel athletic again.

I did the workout with the regulars on my lunch break in my street clothes. Changing in and out of sweats would have taken as long as the exercise itself. Dick found my choice of bell-bottom blue jeans as distasteful as my long, curly hair; but he imposed no dress code—probably because he got a great deal of mileage out of teasing me about my "Commie" look.

One day some weeks after joining the lunchtime class, I entered to find the gym a maze of cables and lighting equipment. Billy Simmons, a local sportscaster, wanted to do a story on Woit and the Warriors. He was going to do the workout, and his camera crew was going to document it. The Bears had left for training camp, so it would be up to the rest of the group to perform.

Dressed in white gym shorts and a Bears jersey, Simmons appeared to be in excellent shape. He was a stocky man in his early forties, with hot-combed blond hair. While the Warriors sat leisurely on the mats snapping their chewing gum, Simmons energetically warmed up for the class by doing jumping jacks.

Dick entered and began his banter early. "Save it for the workout, pretty boy. At this rate, you'll be flat on your ass before the cameras are on. Grab your weights, everybody."

The old black barbells were piled wigwam fashion in the center of the room. On Dick's command, each of the regulars took his weight and put it by the side of his mat. A slightly bewildered Simmons tested several of the remaining barbells. He was about to carry off a 75-pounder when Rod Kosloski, a thirty-five-year-old lawyer, pointed to a 60-pounder with adhesive tape wrapped where one would place one's hands. "Take that one, Billy," he said.

His back to the group as he took off his windbreaker, Dick hadn't seen the scene unfold. Simmons smiled a thank you. But as he leaned over to pick up the weight, Dick kicked him in the back. "You asshole. Nobody touches my weight."

Kosloski, the group's practical joker, who was nicknamed the "Polish Prince," had wisely retreated to a corner and was pretending to tie his shoe. "Hey, Coach," he said, his eyes still to the floor, "do you know what the national sport of Poland is?" The cameras rolling, Dick was not pleased. "Can you believe it, Billy?" he said to Simmons. "This asshole is a lawyer. He's on the thirty-ninth floor of the First National Bank, and he's got a sign in his window that says 'LAWYER 39 FLIGHTS UP.'"

"Thath cauth you'd have to be a pigeon to retain him," came a voice from the corner.

"Very good, Tongue."

Tongue, as Dick called Irv Rosen, was a short, unattractive man in his middle forties. He had made a fortune in condominium conversions and had recently divorced his first wife in favor of a Hawaiian beauty no older than I was. Because he lisped, he rarely spoke out. But now, apparently emboldened by his pigeon line and Simmons's presence, he continued. "Thouldn't we tell Billy to make thure he doethn't hold hith weight upthide down, Coach?"

The barbell was, obviously, symmetrical. There was no up or down. "Tongue," Dick spit, "the only thing 'upthide' down right now is your gook wife. Go call her. I'll lay you fifty to one she's doing it with your chauffeur."

"Are you getting all this down, Billy?" asked Kosloski.

"Shut up, Polack," Dick said. Then to Simmons: "Billy, take your weight and go next to the Crip over there. You'll get used to the smell in a minute. He's a long-haired pig, but I'm betting he's got more balls than you—ready up!"

Dick, the six other regulars, and I were each on our own small rubber mats on top of the large rubber mat in the room. At his command, fourteen legs moved up exactly six inches off the ground. My left leg rose a few inches while my weaker right leg fluttered on and off the mat, a baby bird trying to fly with limited luck.

Unprepared, Simmons had been sitting when the coach issued his order. When he finally put his legs up, they were too high and his rear end was in the middle of the mat. "Get your ass to the edge, Mr. TV, and lower your legs. Jesus, cheating already."

We did four of these "leg-ups," one minute each, with only five seconds rest in between. The exercise demanded strong stomach muscles. Mine were still very weak, as was my right leg, which could only withstand the first thirty seconds of the first set. I concentrated on keeping my left leg airborne. By the second set, Simmons's neck had turned beet red and his legs were shaking. By the third set, despite his obvious effort, his legs were dipping to the floor about every ten seconds. "My stomach feels like it's been stretched to Evanston," he whispered to me. Dick heard this, as he heard everything said or whispered in his shrine. "Evanston's not so bad, Billy. Few more minutes I'll have you up to Milwaukee."

After the leg-ups, we did sixty half sit-ups (I could only do about thirty) and then three more leg-ups, this time ninety seconds each. "You didn't tell me you had palsy, Billy," Dick laughed, reacting to the sportscaster's quivering body. "Just try and keep up with the Crip."

"Don't quit," I whispered. "Just keep trying and you're fine."

"Shut up, Jew. Okay, push-ups."

We threw our mats into the center of the room and put our legs up on the orange benches that stood about sixteen inches off the ground. This Woit push-up was much harder than a conventional one because it required supporting the full weight of your body on your arms. I had trouble just getting my legs on the bench and always raced the clock to achieve the starting position before Dick began the count. We did five sets of fifteen. Dick counted the first ten of each set at a normal pace, the last five excruciatingly slowly. I still couldn't dip on my arms like everyone else—the first time I had tried, I'd landed flat on my face—so Dick had me lock my arms, still a difficult proposition, and raise and lower my trunk.

Simmons did the first ten push-ups easily, but began to have trouble when Dick dragged out the count of the five slow ones even longer than usual. His arms trembled, then shook.

"Is there an earthquake in here?" Dick asked. He lifted his left arm up and scratched his head while the rest of us tried to support ourselves on two arms. The ease with which he did this workout—counting out the exercises, exhorting the Warriors when the rest of us barely had enough strength to speak—was what made us follow him. No one, not even the best of the pro athletes, could do this workout perfectly, save Dick. And he did it six times a day.

"Don't quit, Billy," grunted Manny Sokol, a successful CPA in his early fifties. "Raise your ass up in the air if you have to, but don't quit."

"It figures the accountant will tell you how to cheat," said Dick.

Raising one's ass did make the push-ups easier, taking some of the weight off the arms. Almost everyone adopted the technique at some time during the workout, always risking Dick's wrath. But lifting your ass was preferable to going down to the floor and quitting. Dick simply did not allow quitting. If you gave up, he kicked you out—for good, or in some cases until you begged for another chance. I had already seen one Warrior, a prominent Chicago attorney who I'm sure didn't let anyone push him around in the courtroom, follow Dick like a puppy into the steam room and then the shower pleading for probation, crying while he threw himself on the mercy of the coach.

By the fifth and final set of push-ups, Simmons had perfected the ass-in-the-air trick and was holding on, just waiting for Dick to end the count. A deep puddle of sweat had formed beneath the reporter, and his chin continued to rain more water. "Better not fall, Billy. You'll drown," said Dick, the only person in the room capable of talking at this point. *Five and down. Weights now.*"

Push-ups over, the men rose and moved to their barbells. Simmons sat on the bench to catch his breath. The cameraman moved in for a close-up. "It's not time for a commercial, Billy," Dick rasped. "We're still on the air. No resting. Grab your weight."

While the Warriors struggled through four sets of ten curls and five presses with the free weights, I remained on the floor for more sit-ups and my leg-bending exercise. I could now pull my right leg up several more inches, even without the threat of Dick's kick.

In a way, I missed the special attention I had received during the first six weeks at the gym, but I realized that my inclusion in the group was a sign that I was getting stronger. The Warriors had welcomed me from the beginning, and they still stumbled over each other to help—be it by handing me a weight, spotting me during my hamstring exercise against the wall, or lifting me from mat to bench.

When Dick didn't call me Crip, he called me Stevie. The Warriors all called me Stevie, too. I had abhorred this nickname as a young boy—because it made me sound like a baby. And I abhorred it now for the same reason. At New Trier, the responsibility for guarding the doors to the lunchroom had fallen upon the school jocks, mostly football players. Joining them was one decidedly nonathletic classmate, a boy with a congenital spinal problem that necessitated walking with the same kind of crutches I now used. Everyone called this boy Ricky, although he referred to himself as Rick. Cute, helpless Ricky became a mascot of sorts for the football team and the entire school. I did not want to become a mascot for the Warriors.

Simmons managed to get partway through the first two sets of weights, then stood holding onto the barbell. "My wrists," he moaned.

Everyone complained about the strain on their wrists. "Coach," Manny Sokol had once said, "the feeling I get when I finally get to put my weight down is as good as any sexual thrill I've ever had."

"No wonder you don't have any kids," Dick responded.

After the weights, we all struggled back to the benches for another five sets of push-ups, then another session with the weights, and a final five sets of push-ups, bringing the total number to 225. On the last set of push-ups, Simmons raised his rear end to even greater heights. Dick refused to continue the count, "until Billy reenters the earth's atmosphere." Everyone was struggling now, and each second of delay intensified the pain. The initial sympathy for Simmons turned to rancor. "C'mon, Billy, goddammit," gasped Kosloski, "he'll make us wait all day."

Simmons lowered his ass. "That's it. Just three more, Billy. Why don't you pick out one you like and join us," laughed Dick. Simmons did the next two. One more to go. Dick opened his mouth as if to count, then closed it. Simmons moaned and collapsed. "*And down.*" Dick looked at Simmons. "You quit on me."

"Is that it?" Simmons groaned from the floor.

"Hell, no. We go out to the parking lot and run wind sprints now. C'mon, Billy, it's you versus the Crip. My money's on the Crip." Actually, while the men ran their twelve wind sprints outside, I sat on a bench doing my curls.

Simmons struggled after the Warriors when they ran out and struggled in behind them when they returned several minutes later. After three more curls—with one interminably long minute between each one—the exercise in masochism was over. Simmons sprawled on the mat, a perfect picture for the camera.

When he finally caught his breath, the sportscaster asked if he could interview me. I nodded, but Dick said. "Wait 'til the Crip finishes the rest of his workout." I still had to do the wall.

Simmons said the crew had to be back at the station in a few minutes. Excited by the prospect of my first television appearance, I boldly told Dick that I would only be a little while. The coach didn't answer. He turned around and began to organize the weights on the floor. He remained silent during the interview as well.

The crew finally left, but Simmons and a few of the regulars remained in the gym as I prepared for my hamstrings-against-the-wall routine.

"So now you're a TV star, huh, Crip?" Dick said. "You were pretty smooth. If your legs worked half as well as your mouth, you'd be in the Olympics. Have you looked in the mirror lately?"

"No. I wouldn't want to break it."

The Warriors laughed. I giggled myself.

Dick addressed my audience as he moved to the wall. "You guys think it's funny?" Then, to me: "Get down on the floor, Crip."

This wasn't in the game plan, but I hurriedly obeyed.

"Now get up."

"On my own?" Someone always helped me.

"On your own. Maybe I should call the cameras back in and have them put this on the news for everyone to see. Motherfuckin' sheeny, you can't even get off the floor by yourself."

"Why don't you lay off him, Coach." It was Chris Wilkins, a stout roofer in his middle forties who had once tried out for the Green Bay Packers.

Dick wheeled around toward Wilkins, put both hands behind his back, and offered his chin. "C'mon, big guy, take your best shot. But make it a good one. 'Cause after you do, I'm gonna beat the shit out of you."

Wilkins, who stood six inches taller and weighed at least one hundred pounds more than Dick, just laughed. But no one else in the room did.

"Chicken, huh?" Dick said. "I figured." He turned to me on the floor. "Go ahead, Crip. Get up."

I inched my way across the mat, put my back to the bench, my elbows up, and pushed. My rear end rose a few inches, but I couldn't get up.

"You see what a piece of shit you are. Why don't you do your family a favor and get hit by a car. Or catch cancer. Here, I'll help you over to that window so you can jump out and end it all. You think you're a big deal because they put you on TV? What are they gonna put under your name on the screen? 'Cripple'?" He lifted me back onto the bench and walked out.

Chris Wilkins handed me my crutches. "He doesn't mean it, Stevie."

Everyone else was silent as I left the gym. Down in the locker room, Dick ordered, "Come to my office, Crip."

I followed him down a grimy hall to a small unmarked room with a frosted-glass door. He sat at a standard-issue metal desk. A photo of the coach in his Detroit Lions uniform hung on one wall. Dick at twenty-five was barely recognizable. He weighed forty pounds more than today; his neck was thick, his arms huge. Small crucifixes had been affixed to two other walls. Dick stood beside his parents in another picture.

I stood uneasily, waiting for the next barrage of insults, as Dick reached under his desk. "Here, Crip." He handed me a gray T-shirt with a drawing of a lightning bolt and the words WOIT'S WARRIORS emblazoned in purple.

I fought not to cry. The public tongue-lashing in the gym hadn't bothered me, just as getting thrown off the bench and kicked in the leg hadn't bothered me. I knew that Dick was playing mind games, trying to make me so mad that I'd work even harder to get stronger. I didn't think I needed to be angry at him or the world or God to keep fighting, but I wasn't going to question his techniques. They were working. He could kick me once and kick me twice and kick me once again. It had been a long time since I had bent my right leg. He could wish cancer and the ten plagues upon me on national television. These were such small prices to pay to have my body back. I would gladly have flunked out of college, knocked five years off the end of my life, sacrificed my dog—for my body.

But if the constant verbal abuse and occasional physical assaults didn't make me want to cry, this presentation of a $5 T-shirt did. Only a handful of Dick's men wore the lightning bolt. I had heard Warriors wonder aloud when they would be anointed, whine when others they deemed less deserving had been chosen. What can I compare this to? It outweighed receiving a sports letter in high school or college, was more important than getting into the fraternity you coveted. It was, to those of us seemingly normal people who willingly let a tiny sociopath be our ruler, the equivalent of being knighted.

"You're doing fine, Crip," Dick said after handing me the shirt. "But, you know, I can't go soft in front of the guys. I'd lose their respect." I pictured the Wizard of Oz behind the curtain scaring everyone. "Besides," he continued, "I don't want you getting a big head just because some reporter interviews you. There's only one thing that's important." He pointed to the crutches. "Getting rid of those things."

I started to move forward, to shake his hand, to touch him in some way. But he stopped me. "Now get out of here. You can wear the shirt, but if you ever tell anyone what I just said, I'll break your neck for you a second time."

Simmons's report on the gym aired on that night's ten o'clock news. A few minutes later, our phone rang. "Stevie," Dick said, "I need you to do me a favor. My mom saw the story about us, and she thinks I'm too mean to you. Talk to her, will ya. Here she is."

Mrs. Woit was crying. "That's not my Richard," she told me. "He's the sweetest boy in our parish. He's not really that mean to you, is he?"

Leverage at last. I held the Coach's domestic future in my hands. I could make his life with his mother as difficult as he made my life. "He's not mean at all, Mrs. Woit," I said. "You know you can't believe what you see on television. Your son is the greatest thing to happen to me in years. He's a nice guy."

After that, Dick didn't yell at me for one full workout. He was, however, back on my case the day after that. "Goddamm it, Stevie," he said as I entered the gym. "Your fellow crips are coming out of the woodwork. I got a dozen calls from freaks who saw you on TV and think I can save them, too. There's one coming in today after we're done."

As the workout ended, a small dark-haired man in his late forties shuffled to the doorway. One side of his thin face sagged. His right arm was strapped across his chest in a blue sling. *Stroke victim,* I said to myself. I recognized the type from the Rehab Institute.

Dick signaled for me to stay after the workout, then he asked the man his name.

"Caaarl," the man said. His response sounded more like a yawn than a word.

"Well, Caaarl," Dick mimicked. "Get your ass on the mat and show me how many sit-ups you can do."

Carl obeyed. He did ten sit-ups without too much difficulty. His trunk was much stronger than mine.

"Not bad," Dick said. "Now I want you to do ten more. But this time I want you to count."

Carl nodded. "Onn, twooo, foah—"

"Start over," said Dick. "You missed three."

"Onn, twooo, tree, foah, fi, sen—"

"Start over. You missed six."

He missed "five" on the next try and "six" on the try after that.

"I got all day, Carl," Dick said without any emotion. "We can do this 'til your ass starts bleeding, or you can make it easy on yourself and do it right this time."

Four tries later, Carl did it right. Dick watched him struggle to his feet and then directed him to the wall. "Take off your sling," the coach instructed.

Carl's arm hung lifeless by his side.

"Now climb the wall with your hand, like this," Dick said.

He demonstrated for Carl to inch his fingers up the wall just like the Itsy-Bitsy Spider climbed up the garden spout.

Carl put a closed fist on the wall at about shoulder level.

"Open your hand," said Dick.

Carl's response was unintelligible.

"Wait here," Dick said. He jogged out of the room. When he returned a minute later, he held a book in his hand. "Now try opening your hand again."

Carl tried and failed. Dick whacked the hand against the wall. Splat went the Itsy-Bitsy Spider.

Carl never returned to the gym. Dick's analysis was simple. "He didn't want it bad enough."

. . .

I did want it. Given the choice, I would have preferred to recover without sacrificing our beagle Lefty or flunking out of college or giving up five years of my life. I was, however, more than willing to defer what would have been my junior year at Yale to stay home and continue working out with Dick. My parents supported my decision. The school promised to save my spot and give me credit for an English course I proposed to take at Chicago's Roosevelt College. And Dick told me that if I had gone back to New Haven in the fall, I would have shown I was "even dumber than everyone thinks you are."

With my friends away, I fell into a boring, albeit rewarding, routine. Part-time work at the Rehab Institute two days a week. Nineteenth-century British literature at Roosevelt three days a week. And exercise with Woit's Warriors five days a week. As I knew few people in town and the opportunities for making new friends were limited, I rarely dated. Unwittingly, I was becoming the ascetic that my guru was. Looking back, perhaps I realized that, like Dick, I had to focus all my energy on the workout if I was going to survive.

Dick did invent a game that at least made my Fridays exciting. By December, I had improved to the extent that I did the entire workout—as best I could—alongside the Warriors. Rather than remain on the mats while they did the weights, I hoisted myself up to the bench—*all by myself*—and joined the men for the routine. (I used the lightest barbell available, 30 pounds, and could only do a handful of the curls and presses). I did not go out and run wind sprints, but did walk around the gym crutchless, holding onto the wall when necessary (which was quite often). I still concluded my day at the gym with a set of curls while seated on the bench. Dick would hand me a weight and count out three sets of ten.

That is, Dick was supposed to hand me a weight. One Friday he dropped the weight across my thighs. While this didn't hurt as much as my fall on my face, I can honestly say: it hurt! As I hobbled out of the gym, Dick smiled, "Now you'll remember me 'til Monday." I wanted to say that I would remember him anyway, but wisely kept my mouth shut.

He was right. Confined to bed Saturday and limited to short walks around the house on Sunday because of the pain, I kept Dick in my thoughts constantly. Thereafter, every Friday, Dick tried to drop the weight on me while I tried to catch it before it hit my thighs. Fortunately, I won most of the time. (I harbor no illusions that I was superior here; I know that he let me prevail.)

As I continued to get stronger, Dick began to hint that I should abandon the crutches for a cane. To me, however, the middle of an icy Chicago winter did not seem the ideal time to forgo half of my support system. *Maybe in the spring,* I thought.

March arrived. The ice melted. And I developed a giant lump on my right forearm. Egg-shaped, egg-sized, the growth had materialized out of nowhere. I pressed it, then tried to squeeze it like a pimple, but it was fleshy and unpoppaple.

"Maybe it's the cancer Woit keeps wishing on you," said Jim.

During my first two years away at college, my younger brother had played the same position I had in soccer, debated, edited the yearbook, applied to Yale, and become increasingly sarcastic. In other words, he had become frighteningly like me. I loved him! I envied him, too, for he was now enjoying the senior year that I had never had, or at least completed.

Jim had been hanging out with me and my friends regularly since the accident. He had even taken my place on the Sherman Cartage softball team. Now, in my friends' absence, we spent a great deal of time together playing cards, going to movies, and going to sporting events. Some players on the Chicago Bulls had started working out with Dick, so I had easy access to good basketball seats as well as football tickets.

Jim and I had gone to a Bears game on a bone-chilling day late in the season. Snow started falling early in the second quarter, and by the time we headed out of Wrigley Field for the Malibu, the sidewalk was carpeted with icy crystals. I kept moving forward using my left crutch, but picked up my right crutch and used Jim's shoulder for balance on my weaker side. As we neared the car, Jim raced ahead with me in tow. Briefly. I quickly fell to the ground—uninjured, but stunned that he'd forgotten I was holding on. At least I think he'd forgotten and wasn't paying me back for that day I had tripped him long ago.

I tumbled right in front of a foursome of young men who looked big enough, if not sober enough, to be playing for the

Bears themselves. "Hey, asshole," one of them yelled at Jim through a black and orange woolen face mask. "Ya knocked dat guy over." Then, he looked at me. "Hey, pal. Want us to take care of him?" One of his chivalrous friends showed no interest in waiting for an answer. He moved on Jim as purposefully as a defensive end moving in on a quarterback.

The quarterback looked to me for help. For a moment, I considered letting him suffer the consequences of his actions. Instead, I yelled, "No. Wait. Leave him alone. He's my brother."

I hoped the brother whom I had saved in the parking lot would be joining me in New Haven the coming fall. Without even asking him, I'd sent off a letter of recommendation—a letter much easier to write, physically at least, than my own dictated college essays right after the accident. "I can best describe Jim as a man-child," I told the Yale Admissions Office. I went on to say that he was still a boy in all the positive ways that word could be interpreted; he was shy, naive, unjaded, open, a tabula rasa who would benefit greatly from the Yale experience. At the same time, circumstances beyond his control had forced him to grow up and adopt a very adult role in our family—a role he had handled skillfully and without complaint or self-pity. I left out the part about his being sarcastic.

I squeezed the new growth on my arm again. "It's not cancer, but it probably is contagious," I said to Jim. "And you'll catch whatever it is."

"We're going to the doctor," said my mother.

"It's a ganglion cyst, a loose bundle of nerves. Nothing to worry about," said the doctor.

"It's from that cuff on your crutches," said Dick. "If you

were a man, you'd get rid of them. You don't need them anymore."

Dick's theory didn't make sense. The cuff was two inches from the bump. But I knew the game he was playing: challenge Stevie's manhood and he'll do anything. I also knew that the Coach wouldn't suggest something so dramatic if he didn't really believe I was ready for a cane.

I went home and took out the cane my grandmother had used when she had come to our house to die from cancer—a thick, yellow, hooked wooden stick with a wide rubber suction tip. Cane in left hand, Jim on my right side, I walked back and forth in the living room until bedtime. This time he didn't desert me. By the time I finished, I had beat a path into the white pile carpet.

When I woke up the next morning, a steady rain was falling. "It's too slippery," said my mother as I prepared to leave for the gym. I debated whether to postpone my venture. No. I would always be able to find some excuse for delaying this.

The short stairway from our front door to the driveway was easy. The railing supported me as my missing crutches would. But the rain-soaked asphalt was slicker and bumpier than I realized. I took tiny steps until I reached the front of the Malibu, then leaned on the hood for support until I reached the car door.

The sidewalk outside the gym was particularly slippery. I balanced my free right arm on the fence outside the YMCA parking lot and then the building itself until I was safely inside, where I neglected to figure that the rubber cane tip would be so wet that I would slip forward across the lobby's linoleum floor. Fortunately, the Y's information desk stood between me

and disaster; I was able to grab onto it and regain my balance.
I dried the tip and proceeded up to the gym.

Moving with such caution had made me late; a sin almost
as deadly as an unexcused absence. When I entered the gym,
the Warriors were already on the mats. Dick looked up. I knew
he saw the cane, but just to make sure, I set it loudly against
the wall.

"You're late, Crip."

"Hey, congratulations," said Chris Wilkins as I lowered myself to the floor.

"Quiet," shot Dick.

The Coach didn't acknowledge the cane during the workout
or in the locker room.

"Don't you notice anything different about Stevie today?"
asked Kosloski.

"No. Oh, wait a second. Did you finally take a shower,
Crip?"

.   .   .

I can't say for sure whether it was the confidence I was feeling having shed the crutches a few days earlier or the sense
that I was getting closer to normal that moved me to pick up
the young girl hitchhiking in front of a Tudor mansion on
Sheridan Road a few miles from my home; I might very well
have picked her up anyway. I am certain, however, that the
giddiness I had felt since starting on the cane emboldened me
to plan a romantic evening with her that I hoped would end in
the bedroom. (I cannot overestimate the psychological effect
of getting rid of the crutches. This was like getting rid of the
training wheels on a bike, like learning to and daring to catch
a high fly ball with one hand rather than two, in the fashion

of Rickey Henderson today. On the crutches, I had become the sommelier of the sidewalks. My eyes fixed on the ground, I could tell you that a ZANE PAVING COMPANY 1965 had a nice smooth finish, where a MOORE, INC. 1966 was a little rough around the edges. I'd have been a rich man, too, if only I could have bent down to pick up all the loose change I saw on the pavement.)

On the cane, I began to develop the confidence to look up, ahead of me. Admittedly, looking forward instead of down had the unpleasant consequence of revealing how many people, particularly children, stared at me as I walked among them. But this was not really a surprise. I had "heard" them staring all along. Heard children ask their parents what was wrong with me, heard parents whisper back not to look—lest like Lot's wife they be turned to a pillar of salt, I guess. Although I refused to look in mirrors or windows to watch myself walk (and closed my eyes if I appeared on screen in a home movie), I figured I looked healthier on a cane than on crutches—although at age twenty, I actually heard a few children refer to me as an "old man"—so the staring didn't bother me. Indeed, sometimes when I caught a child's eye, I would smile and give the cane a Chaplinesque twirl. If I was lucky, I'd demystify myself and the child would smile back. When not so lucky, I'd almost literally shoot myself in the foot—losing my balance and having to stutter step to regain it.

The hitchhiking girl exposed to this newfound confidence was named Daphne. She was seventeen, three years younger than I was, a senior at New Trier like Jim. But unlike Jim, who was following the same achievement-directed path that I had followed, Daphne was laid-back, if not stoned. As we drove north along Sheridan, the lake glistening to our right, she spoke slowly and fiddled endlessly with her long dishwater blond hair. She wore a long denim skirt with patches, earth shoes, and a flowered headband. She wasn't particularly attractive—she called to mind a younger, softer version of Janis Joplin, whom I had seen perform at Yale my sophomore year—but I was home, horny, newly on the cane, and my parents and brothers were leaving for Bermuda in two days. I asked for her phone number when I dropped her at her home about a mile from our house. "Call me soon," she said as she gave it to me.

I hadn't insinuated myself onto this spring vacation—not only because of the bad memories of the last family getaway, but because I didn't want to take any time away from the gym. Having the house to myself, I quickly called Daphne and invited her over. After she said yes, I prepared for an evening of romance by brushing my teeth and removing my leg bag. I figured we wouldn't be going out and that when nature called I could make it to the bathroom at home with time to spare.

Daphne arrived in her parents' car after dinner. If I had been at school, I would have been lucky to find some American cheese and muscatel in our mini–ice box. Fortunately, my parents' refrigerator offered wine and cheese better suited for seducing. I appropriated some Jarlsberg and a bottle of chardonnay. We listened to music and made out on the family room couch, and then, my heart pounding, I suggested we head upstairs. That was fine with her.

I had also appropriated my parents' bedroom while they were away, because it had a phone. Conveniently, the room featured a king-sized bed. Soon Daphne and I were under the covers naked.

I had always imagined that I would share my first sexual experience with a girl I loved, a girl beautiful in spirit and body. I didn't love Daphne. I didn't know her well enough to pass judgment on her spirit. She was not a great beauty. Having gotten this far, however, I was not going to let details like these stand in my way.

Daphne was not much more experienced than I was. Our sex would have been awkward even without my inability to move hands, and legs, and torso with spontaneity and abandon. As I had imagined, performance was difficult, but it was not, as I had often feared, impossible. I fell asleep certain that I would have no qualms about having sex again with Daphne or anyone else for whom I had little feeling, but still uncertain if I would have the confidence to risk making love to someone for whom I really cared.

CHAPTER 14

"I don't think you should wear a suit," I said to my father. "This isn't a suit crowd." I turned to Jim. "And I don't think you should be wearing blue jeans. It's a little more formal than that."

"What about me?" my mom asked as she came into the family room. She was wearing a long black skirt and a short-sleeved white blouse.

"You're fine," I said. "But these two." I pointed at Dad and Jim as I struggled with my tie—a regular one, not a clip-on. Can somebody help me with this goddamn thing before I rip it in half," I said.

"You help him, Elaine," Dad said. "Jim and I have to go up-stairs and change. We don't want to cross the Coach."

"Is that what you want us to call him, 'Coach'?" Mom asked as we neared the Y. "Gee, I didn't realize what a crummy neighborhood this was."

"I'm not usually here at night," I said. "And besides, there's a parking lot right next to the building."

"So is it 'Coach'?" Dad asked. "Or Mr. Woit—"

"Or *Dick*," said Jim.

I elbowed him in the stomach, knowing he'd be afraid to return the favor. "'Coach' is fine," I said. "And remember, no smoking once we get inside. Also . . ." I paused.

"Yes?" said Dad.

"Well, I don't know how to put this, but if Dick tells you you're a fat piece of shit and that if you don't work out you'll be dead in six months, try to ignore him."

"I've heard worse," Dad said. "At home."

I knew he was talking to me. "Well, you should work out," I stammered. I had to admit that tonight, however, my concern was not for my father's health. I didn't want him to be embarrassed by the always blunt Coach. I didn't want to be embarrassed either.

I had tried to imagine what my father and my coach might talk about. Did they share any passions? Not food. Dad, the gourmand, searched out new restaurants and recipes—and his waistline showed it. Dick had never demonstrated an interest in anything other than Cool Whip—and his waistline showed it. Wine? My father had built a cellar in the basement and was assembling an impressive collection. Dick didn't know a Chateau Mouton-Rothschild from Morty Rothschild, an actuary who worked out in the four o'clock class. Travel? Dad had decided it was time to go to Europe, the Orient, Russia. Dick said the only place he dreamed of going was Las Vegas. Cars? Dick spent hours every week waxing his beloved Oldsmobile Toronado. Dad took his Buick Riviera to the nearby car wash. Music? Dad's current obsession was taping symphonies and operas from the local classical music station. I teased that he spent so much time on his filing system for the completed tapes that he would never have the chance to listen to the music. Dick's idea of the *Goldberg Variations* was the difference in push-up technique between Stu Goldberg from the ten-fifteen class and Howie Goldberg from the two o'clock.

All was not lost, however. Gardening was a possibility. Dick mowed his lawn and the lawn of all of the aging members of his parish in the neighborhood. Dad spent long hours in the yard tending to his flowers and bushes. No, I thought. Best not to bring up bushes. Maybe movies. Dick loved Westerns, and so did my father. Yes, movies.

We walked through the humid August night from the parking lot to the Y's stark lobby, where the announcement board proclaimed WELCOME WOIT'S WARRIORS—FIRST ANNUAL AWARDS BANQUET. WASHINGTON ROOM. FIRST FLOOR.

The Washington Room was about ten yards down the hall. As we headed in its direction, we were joined by Manny Sokol, the accountant. A striking redhead somewhere between my age and Jim's walked beside Manny, towered over him actually, in three-inch heels. Her white miniskirt barely reached beyond her crotch. You could see right through her sheer white top. "Hey, Stevie," Manny said. "This is Julie."

"Stevie?" Dad whispered as we continued down the hall.

"I can't believe it," Mom said, motioning her head in Julie's direction. "I almost wore that very same outfit."

I laughed nervously, but Jim was stone silent. He was still trying to get a good look at Julie.

Dick/Coach/Mr. Woit was standing by the entrance to the room. He wore a maroon sport coat over a yellow shirt with a wide collar. No tie. His shiny black slacks were about an inch too high. "Hey, Crip," he called.

"Crip?" Dad whispered.

"Dick, you met my brother Jim a couple of times. These are my parents."

"Hey, pleased to meet you," he said, smiling. He shook each one's right hand with both of his.

"Dad," I said, "Coach loves Clint Eastwood as much as you do."

"We have a mutual friend," Dad said to Dick, ignoring me. "Charlie Horton."

"For Chrissakes," said Dick. "Charlie and I played sixteen-inch softball for years."

"So I hear," Dad said. "He says you were the best."

"Not too shabby," Dick said.

A waitress came by with a tray of fresh shrimp and cocktail sauce. "You guys like shrimp?" Dick asked. "This is good stuff. One of my guys in the three o'clock—you know Eddie Viglione, Crip?—he distributes these. Crab claws, too."

Dick grabbed a shrimp off the plate and ate it. Almost every night at dinner, I provided a report of the colorful doings at the gym and Dick's eccentricities—including the fact that he only ate Cool Whip. Now Dad, Jim, and Mom looked at me quizzically.

I took a shrimp and started to dip it in the sauce.

"I wouldn't do that, Crip," Dick said. "Cocktail sauce, ketchup, they cut down on your wind."

"I didn't know we were doing the workout tonight," Kosloski interrupted. He held the arm of an older woman in a red dress. Her hair was dyed a strange shade of brown; her makeup was excessive; and she was smoking a cigarette. "Your Ma wanted to talk to you, Coach," Kosloski said.

"I really wanted to meet Stevie," Mrs. Woit said. "Richard tells me all about you."

Tongue Rosen, his beautiful Hawaiian wife in tow, came out to complain that the bartender was watering down the drinks. Dick excused himself, leaving us with his mother. She soon departed to find Dick's father. Jim said he wanted to get a Coke, but I was sure he just wanted to get another look at Julie. Mom followed him.

"Stevie?" Dad asked when we were alone. "Crip?"

"Charlie Horton?" I countered.

"I did my homework," he said, smiling.

The banquet started a few minutes later. The London broil, courtesy of Stosh the meat guy in the ten o'clock class, was better than expected. The cheesecake, courtesy of Freddy from the eleven-thirty, was also excellent. I watched Dick up on the dais. He didn't eat the meat or the dessert, but he did eat several pieces of shrimp—no sauce.

He needed his wind. After dinner he stood up and talked. First, he thanked us all for coming. Next, he acknowledged his parents. Then, he said, "I'm not joking when I say what an honor it is to be surrounded by some of Chicago's best lawyers, doctors, bankers, contractors, cops, and even bookies." He paused and looked at Bobby N. from the four o'clock.

"I never married," Dick continued. "You know it wouldn't be fair to a woman."

"That's for sure," heckled Kosloski.

"I'm not even going to answer that—tonight," Dick said. "What I mean to say is that besides my mom and dad, you're my family."

Then, he said that, "growing up with all the Polacks on the Northwest Side," he expected he might get to go to banquets at the White Eagle Hall in the neighborhood, but never dreamed that he'd be hosting an affair like tonight.

"I never dreamed I'd get out of the neighborhood in my whole life. Period," he said. "But the good Lord gave me the ability to run with a football good enough so that some coach from Arkansas State was willing to pay me to go to his college. And then the good Lord let me play well enough down there so that the Detroit Lions wanted me to carry the football for them. And then after Korea, I did. And if you think that wasn't a thrill. When I was a rookie, they assigned me to room with Bobby Layne. For those of you who don't know who Bobby

Layne was—he was a great quarterback and an even greater drinker and cocksman, if you'll pardon the expression. I was supposed to be the guy who kept him in check. Instead, I learned a thing or two from him.

"Those were great days, but then the good Lord saw fit to make a guy named Emlen Tunnell of the New York Giants tackle me so hard I ended up in a coma for two days and needed a steel plate in my head. I tell ya, when I came back to Chicago, I thought I was gonna sell shoes for the rest of my life. Shoes or sporting goods. Maybe play some softball. But then I got a call from a guy who knew a guy who knew the Y here was looking for an instructor and boom—here I am. I wouldn't trade my life with anybody. I get to be with all you guys, share your lives, meet your . . . meet your whatevers, families, and I get to help people. People like Gale, that's Gale Sayers, when he came here a few years ago."

He spoke for another ten minutes, then began presenting the awards. Every Warrior was recognized for some accomplishment and Dick said something nice about each one as he handed them their trophies. An hour later only one trophy—the largest by far—remained on the table. And only one Warrior remained trophyless. Me.

"I met Stevie's parents tonight," Dick began. "His father's a nice guy—too fat—but a nice guy. His mother. Brother. They're a nice family. A lot of you remember when Stevie came here. He was in a wheelchair, couldn't do much more than blink his eyes. I made him stand up. And then I made him use crutches. And then when I thought he was ready I picked up the crutches and threw 'em out the window. True story."

"Wheelchair?" my father whispered.

"Blink?" Mom said.

"Out the window?" Jim asked.

"True story. True story. True story," I said, trying to stifle a smile.

"And now if Stevie would come up here."

I stood up slowly, took my cane and walked from our table in the middle of the hall up toward the dais. There wasn't much room to manuever between all the other tables and chairs. The last thing I wanted to do was take a header. I moved cautiously.

"Isn't that beautiful, the way he moves," Dick said proudly. "As beautiful as a Gale Sayers run."

People started applauding.

"I'll tell you," Dick continued over the clapping. "When I first saw Stevie, I wasn't sure he wanted it bad enough. Well, I made sure he did. And now? What is it, fifteen months later? He's going back to that cow college of his in Connecticut or some place in a few weeks, but if he does what I tell him to do, I promise he'll be running wind sprints with all the rest of the Warriors this time next summer."

I had reached the dais. The applause was getting louder and then everyone was on their feet. Dick handed me the trophy. "I can't carry this," I whispered. "It's too heavy. I'll drop it." He set it back on the table.

"One last thing," Dick said. "I know I'm never going to have a son of my own, but if I did, I'd be happy if he was just like Stevie. God bless you, Crip."

There wasn't a dry eye in the house. Not Dick's. Not my parents'. Not mine.

.   .   .

Four weeks later, after almost a year and a half in Dick Woit's boot camp, I was ready for my honorable discharge. I had lost twenty-five pounds and my crutches while regaining my self-respect and confidence. I felt special, superior to those outside the Warrior clan, for having endured the workout and earned my leader's respect.

As the summer of 1971 came to an end, Dick would occasionally tell me that I was making a mistake by going back to New Haven. But he knew that my departure was not only inevitable but appropriate. I had promised to pack a set of weights and a bench so that I could continue the regime at school. Of course, I would return to the gym on vacations and for the next summer. Dick repeated his prediction that if I kept at it, I'd be off the cane and running within a year. I believed him.

On my last day at the gym, I gave him an elegant silver pocket watch.

"It's beautiful, Crip," he said. "I wish I could keep it. But I'm not a pocket watch kind of guy. I'd never use it. Do you think you could exchange it for a regular wristwatch?"

"I'm leaving for school tomorrow, Dick."

"What about this afternoon?"

The jewelry store where I'd bought the watch was only a ten-minute cab ride away. I made the exchange and returned to the gym. Dick was in his office.

"Don't get me wrong, Crip. This one's nice, too. But look how big the dial is. I got small wrists."

"Listen," I said, holding back my annoyance, "the store isn't too far from here. Maybe you could go and pick out something you really like."

"Shit, Crip. You're going out like you came in—a failure."

He pulled open a desk drawer and took out an unwrapped cardboard box. "I got you something, too. This is for school."

He opened the box to reveal a digital clock-radio. "Now, no excuse for missing classes or your workout, huh?"

I started to cry. Dick's thrift was legendary. I had never heard of him giving anything to anyone besides a Warriors T-shirt (which, I learned, Herbie, a clothing guy in the ten-fifteen class, provided him free of charge).

Dick hugged me, then kissed me on the cheek. "Okay, scram, Crip. I'll see you at Thanksgiving. And if you put on one pound or can't do the fucking workout, don't bother to show your ugly face around here."

On my way out of the Y, I ran into Jimmy H., a Warrior in the two o'clock who worked at one of the city's biggest radio stations. "Where'd you get the radio, Stevie?"

"Coach gave it to me."

Jimmy H. laughed.

"What's so funny?" I asked.

"Nothing. It just looks a lot like the freebie I gave him yesterday."

PART FOUR

Almost all of my Warriors are or have become
achievers. If they weren't successful when they
began, they became successful after developing the
discipline and mental toughness that the workout
automatically gives you. It is the rare person who
can achieve anything without being aware of his or
her body and taking care of it. You must have some
feeling and respect for yourself to maintain your
body or you will be a failure at whatever you do.

from You Gotta Want It! *by Dick Woit*

CHAPTER 15

Here is what I brought back to Yale in September of 1971:
A fifty-pound weight.
A weightlifting bench.
An exercise mat.
My Chevy Malibu.
My brother Jim, who had been accepted into the Class of 1975.
A cane, no crutches.
A Warrior mentality.

.   .   .

"You're different," a friend told me as I walked into the dining hall shortly after I returned to school. "You're carrying yourself like an athlete."

The Yale I returned to for my junior year had, in some ways, changed as dramatically as I had. The student strike was over, and the Panthers no longer prowled the campus. Bobby Seale had pled guilty to a lesser charge.

One thing didn't change. My room in Timothy Dwight College became a salon once again. When I had first come home from the hospital, my friends had been anxious to push themselves around in my wheelchair—a kind of walk (or ride) on the wild side, imagining what it would be like to be injured. They had limped around on my crutches just as eagerly. Now, my friends twirled my thick yellow cane and played with my exercise equipment as I told them stories about Dick Woit and the pro athletes at the Y.

Few classmates believed my tales of the gym. Thus, when my roommate Bob visited me at home over Christmas vacation, I insisted he try the workout so that he could provide an objective report to the skeptics. With perverse glee, I told Dick that Bob was on the crew team at Yale and, therefore, in excellent shape. This was true. The team trained every day throughout the fall and winter—running, lifting weights, rowing in indoor tanks and on the nearby Housatonic River. I had watched the six-foot-tall Bob transform himself from a shy, skinny 150-pounder into a confident, muscled young man.

Bob *looked* more fit than most of the Warriors, many of whom smoked, drank, and ate excessively despite their obsessions about being in perfect shape (or perhaps because they believed that as Warriors they were immune to cancer and heart disease). I knew, however, that no one—no matter what shape he was in—could do the unique Woit workout the first time. The sheer number of repetitions and the short period between intervals preordained a newcomer's failure. I also knew that, prepped with information about my roommate, Dick would put on a show for him—and the rest of us.

Midway through the second set of push-ups, as Bob, his face flush, struggled to remain on his quaking arms, Dick shook his head: "I've seen girls do better push-ups than that; hell, your crip roommate even does 'em better than you." Later, when Bob switched from a 70-pound barbell to a 50-

pounder for the final round of presses and curls, the Coach snarled, "Yale, huh? Do they even have a football team there?" And finally, as Bob, his hair wet with snow, ice dripping from his nose, straggled in from the wind sprints and collapsed onto a bench, Dick had asked, "Any jerkoff here really think crew is a sport?"

While I may have looked athletic to my friends, not everyone agreed. Early in my senior year, I phoned to invite a girl from Manhattanville College to a football game. Her slurred speech suggested she had been drinking heavily. I forged ahead anyway. Apparently thinking I was someone else, she proceeded to tell me about this guy she had met at Yale and how she regretted giving him her phone number because "he was crippled."

Crippled. I was devastated—not because I wouldn't be seeing the girl again, but because she felt this horrid term was relevant. I was far from running windsprints, but I was stronger than ever. I had exercised faithfully at school and with Dick when I had come home for the summer of 1972. Despite the year away from the Y, my workout had improved; I could handle more weight and do more push-ups. More important, this strength had been translated into increased mobility; I still needed the cane to negotiate distances and changes in level outdoors, but I could get around the house or my college room now without any assistance, leaning on walls and chairs and anything else I could find to do-si-do from one place to the next.

Crippled. It was one thing to hear Dick Woit use the word to psyche me up; it was something else to hear a girl use it to describe me dismissively. After catching my breath, I thought about confronting her. But what purpose would that serve? She was not in a state to be enlightened, embarrassed, or chastised. I made up some excuse and hung up the phone without revealing my identity. Then I drank enough muscatel to make *me* forget who I was.

At a party a week later, however, I met a girl who didn't call me a cripple or make me want to forget who I was. Her name was Kyla Borden, and I fell in love with her on our first date—when she asked me to dance. We were having dinner at a Hungarian restaurant that I selected not for its tolerable goulash or mediocre five-piece orchestra, but because of its first-rate accessibility; there were no stairs. (I tried to plan first dates at places where I wouldn't have to show any physical weakness.)

In the five years since I had been hurt, no girl had ever asked me to dance. When Kyla, a tall, shapely blonde who was one of the brightest, prettiest girls at Yale, took my hand as the orchestra played "Yesterday," I would have followed her anywhere.

I had known about Kyla since she had arrived on campus with the first wave of coeds in the fall of 1969. One of my sophomore classmates had spent more time with the face book featuring the just-arrived freshmen than with any assigned textbook. He had painstakingly compiled a "Top Ten Co-ed" list, ranking Kyla number two. Now, three years later and still a "cripple" in the eyes of some women, I found it hard to believe that someone as desirable as Kyla, someone who could have her choice of any guy on campus, might choose me. I quickly adopted what one of my friends called "the Avis strategy." Like the number-two rental car company bucking the odds to win favor, I figured I had to "try harder." I sent Kyla flowers the day after our date, chocolates the day after that, and then a poem in the style of Ogden Nash in which I attempted to humorously reprise our dinner conversation about her interest in astrology and her self-confessed tendency to wear her heart on her sleeve.

As we saw more of each other, I went in to overdrive with a calculated campaign to advertise what I perceived to be my strongest selling point—courage in the face of adversity. Over the years, I had become a master at slyly sneaking in stories about the hospital, the Rehab Institute, and Dick's gym, then responding to the inevitable admiration for my fortitude by adopting an "aw shucks, t'weren't nothin' " attitude. (I had told these stories so many times that I had learned how to make my listener laugh or cry on cue, just as Dick could cause a Warrior to stay up on his arms or fall face first to the floor.) In effect, I tried to move Kyla as unrelentingly as I had tried to move my fingers and toes in the days and weeks following the accident.

Kyla seemed the perfect candidate for such manipulation, for as bright and as beautiful as she was, she lacked, or felt she lacked, both confidence and direction. She was looking for the big picture and, not surprisingly, she couldn't find it.

Shortly after we began seeing each other, she was to meet me in my room after a late-afternoon class. She arrived an hour later than promised, her face flush, her fine hair matted to her forehead, her navy blue peacoat open despite the cold November air.

"I was worried," I said as I opened the door.

She sat down on my couch and began to cry. I moved from my chair and joined her (sitting to her right so that I could use my left hand, which remained superior). She was trembling. I put my arm around her.

"What's wrong?" I asked.

She reached into her coat pocket. "Look at this." She revealed a small grayish-white stone.

I looked at it. I didn't know what to say. It was just a stone to me.

"See how it's shaped like a heart?"

Just barely, I thought. More like the poor imitations I cut out from construction paper on Valentine's Day in grade school. "I guess so," I said. I didn't know where she was heading.

"Doesn't it make you wonder if there's a plan for the universe, for all of us?" she asked.

I thought for a moment before deciding that honesty was the best policy here. "Not really. I haven't given it much thought." I truly hadn't. Maybe I was too busy worrying about getting from point A to point B on Earth; maybe I didn't want to think that my accident was anything but an accident.

"Well, I think about it a lot," she said. "And sometimes not knowing ties me in knots."

Poor Kyla. She was lost. I wanted to help her—as much for my own purposes, I admit, as for hers. For if Kyla Borden wanted me, then the accident would finally be behind me. I could look at myself as whole again. Her love would validate that I was normal. If she could accept me, I could accept myself.

I wiped away the tears that had gathered on her windburned cheeks. I spouted the usual clichés that people always seemed to take as wisdom because I had hit a wrestling mat the wrong way. I told her that she had everything going for her. I told her that things usually worked out for the best. I told her that I would be there for her.

She kissed me on the forehead, then put the stone in my hand. "You've handled what happened to you so beautifully," she said. "I really respect you."

Respect. I hated the word almost as much as I hated *cripple.* I wanted to say, "Thanks, but I'm tired of being respected by everyone. I want to be loved, particularly by you." Instead, I was silent.

The accident had taught me to be patient. I figured that Kyla was smart enough to realize that her life was stormy when it shouldn't have been and that mine appeared remarkably storm-free despite my experiences. Sooner or later, she would see that I could be her rock, her anchor, her *fixer*. The question was: could I become her lover and mate as well?

This question remained not only unanswered, but unasked. Little had changed since my one-night stand with Daphne almost two years earlier. In my mind, sexual spontaneity remained impossible as long as I remained glued to the external catheter and strapped to the leg bag—an arrangement I was reluctant to reveal to my male friends, much less to potential girlfriends. At the same time, sexual confidence remained unattainable as long as I lacked total control of my body. I could orchestrate a one-night stand without revealing the bag. I could survive if I ended up being awkward in bed if it didn't matter if I ever saw the girl again. But I needed a much greater sense of security if I was going to risk such awkwardness with a woman I wanted to see again.

I wanted to see Kyla forever.

.   .   .

Kyla had enough credits to graduate summa cum laude in political science at the end of the semester in January. She planned to backpack through Europe in the summer, so she hoped to spend the winter and spring somewhere she could live cheaply and earn travel money. She was tired of New Haven and didn't want to move to Idaho, where her widowed father had recently relocated.

I didn't want to lose her. I looked at my own transcript. Yale agreed to give me credit for the two advanced placement courses I had taken in high school and for the class I had taken at Roosevelt while in Chicago. I could leave early, too, my dean said, though I'd still have to enroll for the second semester in order to receive two additional credits for the required year-long paper for my American studies major. I phoned my parents with my plan. I'd live at home, finish the paper, work out with Dick, and get a job that would last until I went to law school in the fall.

From the very first time that I had twisted my mother's words to my advantage, everyone who knew me had assumed I would be a lawyer. Through elementary school and junior high, I had accompanied my father to his law office on weekends. I had sat on the bench with judges who were family friends, while lawyers who were also friends argued their cases. I had perfected my own skills in cross-examination across the dinner table from my brother and across the classroom table from high school debate opponents. Watching my father in action during the preceding summer had sealed the deal. He now represented an NFL football team, having fashioned a complicated transaction in which one of his longtime clients, Robert Irsay, had purchased the Los Angeles Rams and then swapped them for the Baltimore Colts.

This had been the most exciting work of his career—not only for him, but for me, the sports junkie and would-be law student. Crisscrossing the country to hammer out the purchase had energized Dad for the first time since his partner Dino's hospitalization. He would return from Los Angeles, New York, or Baltimore bubbling about the latest twists and turns, though always careful not to compromise his client's privacy.

We both sensed that this union of law and sports could serve to unite us as well. This time I read everything he put on my pillow, and we discussed all the legal issues as well as his negotiating tactics. I took the law boards later that summer and completed my applications to several schools during the fall. Stanford and the University of Chicago were my top choices. I hoped to hear from them over the next few months.

My parents endorsed my plan to return home, and Dad quickly found me the perfect job. My hundred-page senior paper, "Transportation and the Elderly and Handicapped," was an extension of the research that I had done at the Rehab Institute. One of my father's old friends, the alderman who headed the Chicago City Council's Transportation Committee, hired me to survey the architectural and transit barriers facing Chicago's disabled—work that would apply to my thesis and, more important, might lead to changes in the city's largely inaccessible public transportation system.

I asked my father if he might be able to find a job for one more person.

"Where would I live?" Kyla asked when I suggested she come to Chicago and work for Dad's firm. He just happened to have mentioned that he needed a messenger, I had told her.

I had anticipated this question, too. "Of course, she can stay with us," my mom had said when I had asked earlier in the week. "But she'll have to stay in Jim's room. I don't want you two living together here. If Tommy weren't so young, I wouldn't care, but . . ." My mother was giving me more credit than I deserved, but I didn't tell her that.

She picked up on it soon after we arrived in late January. It was clear from the way Kyla and I behaved in the house that we were more than friends, but far less than lovers. We held hands, even kissed publicly on occasion, but so often Kyla's manner suggested that she was not content. She seemed afflicted by a combination of melancholy and wanderlust. She would be sitting at the table or on the couch, and all of a sudden she would get a faraway look, wouldn't hear what you were saying, and then her left foot would start tapping—as uncontrollably, it seemed to me, as my spasms after the accident. She didn't seem to be aware of it, but more often than not, a few minutes after the tapping started, she would announce that she needed to take a walk. Sometimes she'd be gone for hours.

I didn't ask if she wanted company and she didn't request any. We both knew that I couldn't keep up with her. Shortly after we had arrived in Glencoe, she had suggested we go on a walking tour of Frank Lloyd Wright homes in suburban Oak Park. I was flattered that she asked; as with dancing, over the past five years, no one had invited me on a *walking* tour.

Our tour began at two o'clock. My tour ended a few minutes later, after it became clear that I wouldn't be able to keep up with the group as they began a long walk that would bring them to several homes. Sleet had begun to fall just as we started. I knew I couldn't fight both the slippery sidewalks and the distances without holding everybody up. "I'll wait for you," I told Kyla.

"Okay," she said. She didn't look back.

I was glad that she wasn't affording me any special treatment.

I was sad that she wasn't affording me any special treatment.

Several weeks later, after Kyla had disappeared on one of her walks, I asked my mother: "What do you think she does?"

Kyla had said she'd accompany me to a memorial service for a friend's mother who had recently died. If she didn't return soon, I'd have to leave without her.

"I don't know. But when she comes back, she doesn't look any less sad than when she left," Mom said. She and Kyla had become quite close. Kyla's relationship with her father and siblings was not strained so much as it was distant. I had begun to believe that the best way to her heart might be through my family—if we showed her what a stable, loving relationship we all had, she'd want to be a Fiffer forever.

She came up the driveway just as I was getting into my car. There was no apology; there never was. A cold March rain was just beginning to fall. "I can be ready quickly," she said. She was bathed in sweat, as she often was after these walks. At various times, I thought it was the sweat of lovemaking. But with whom? Where? I decided it was probably just the cold sweat of confusion. On this day, she had a rose pinned to the lapel of her coat.

"Where'd you get the flower?" I finally said as we approached the hospital where the service was being held. My friend's mother had counseled patients here before succumbing to her own cancer.

"Don't ask," Kyla said firmly.

I didn't.

The shower had become a driving thunderstorm. We pulled into the hospital parking lot. All the spaces in the rows near the entrance were filled, save one.

Kyla spotted it. "There," she said, pointing to the HANDI-CAPPED ONLY sign.

I drove past it.

"What are you doing?"

"I won't park in those spaces."

"Why not?"

"I don't consider myself handicapped. The minute I do, I'll start acting as if I am."

"Steve, it's pouring."

"I can see that."

"This is ridiculous. You do what you want, but let me out."

I did.

The only space I could find was about half a block from the entrance. I was soaked by the time I meet her in the lobby.

"You're a jerk," she said.

Maybe. But I wasn't ready to accept the label "handicapped" any more than I could accept being called "cripple." I saw my body as a work in progress. Like Michelangelo sculpting the lifelike David out of a lifeless block of stone, Dick Woit and I would, I believed, turn me into an equally alive Stevie—caneless, braceless, limpless. To do anything to impede this process—including thinking of myself as handicapped or in need of a special parking space—would have interfered with our artistic vision.

We got to the auditorium just as the service was starting. As we sat down, one of my friends entered our row. "What happened to you?" he asked.

"There were no parking spots."

"I know," he said, climbing over me to get to an empty seat.

"So how come you're not wet?"

He smiled. "I parked in the handicapped space."

.   .   .

I am broiling the two sirloins I picked up at the grocery store earlier in the day. The salad is already tossed and dressed.

The green beans are steaming on the stove. The red wine is breathing—probably more easily than I am.

It is late May, four months since Kyla and I came home from New Haven. Much has happened. I have finished my senior paper. After being turned down by Stanford, I have decided to go to the University of Chicago Law School in the fall. I'm happy with the decision. Most of my friends from childhood have moved back to the city, and I have no qualms about going to my father's alma mater. I've proved myself in college.

Before law school I will travel. Kyla has earned enough money to go to Europe and will soon fly to Stockholm. I will be with her. As the spring has worn on, Kyla has grown increasingly worried about traveling by herself. At the same time, I have grown increasingly certain that I want to be with her. Sharing the European adventure seems the best way to move our relationship to the next level.

We still haven't discussed the relationship, which remains somewhere between friend and lover. I have been reluctant to ask her how she feels about me and about our future. My guess is that she isn't certain yet. I think that if I weren't on the cane, she wouldn't have any doubts. But I am. Asking more of her emotionally or physically might send her off on a walk from which she'd never return. Instead of asking, I have to show.

Europe offers the perfect opportunity to prove myself to her, just as I have proved myself to everyone else who has doubted my abilities. Once there, she will see me as an indispensable source of strength, stability, and comfort, while marveling at my character, courage, and self-confidence in conquering the physical barriers of the continent. (I realize now that this laundry list of adjectives makes me sound less like a boyfriend than a Boy Scout helping a lady in need across a continent. But I realize, too, that I was only twenty-two years old when making these decisions.)

We are to leave in two weeks. So now I set the table and light the candles. My parents are away for the weekend—thus, the carefully planned romantic dinner for two to be followed, I hope, by our very first night of making love. I have prepared myself as well as the meal. I'm freshly showered, sans leg bag.

Lisa arrives on time. Yes, Lisa. Kyla left two weeks earlier to visit her father in Idaho.

I met Lisa at a party two days later. She's in graduate school at Northwestern. She has blond hair, a nice figure, a pleasant face—attractive, but not nearly as attractive as Kyla. She wears a considerable amount of makeup and, unlike almost all of my female contemporaries, has a hairdo, an actual beauty-shop tinted, coiffed, 1950s-like hairdo. She dresses more formally than Kyla, too, in wool skirts, white blouses, dark hose, and heels. But if her feet are in heels rather than work boots, they are also on the ground. I can tell from the few conversations we've had that she's stable and self-confident. In short, she's more adult than Kyla—and for that matter, me.

What's she doing here if I am so in love with Kyla? This isn't getting together for a friendly cup of coffee or a get-to-know-you lunch. I have, I hope, orchestrated a seduction. Why? Because I'm horny. Because I'm frustrated that Kyla and I haven't slept together. Because I want to know if other women find me desirable sexually. Because I want to build up my confidence so that I can tell Kyla I want to make love to her.

When it's over, when Lisa has risen naked from my parents' bed, put on her adult clothes, kissed me, asked when we can get together again, and let herself out the front door, I'm still frustrated. Despite Lisa's reassurances, my performance during this undressed rehearsal for Kyla was less than perfect. What will happen in Europe?

Nothing. In Stockholm, our first stop, I find lodging for us in a private home. When our host offers us a room with a queen-sized bed, Kyla looks at me suspiciously and asks for twin beds.

Later that day, we walk along the canal. After a couple of blocks, I start to fade. By the time we walk another block, I am ten yards behind her, working my hardest to keep up. I feel as if I am part of some weird Scandinavian ritual that dictates that the man must follow several paces behind the woman. Perhaps I should wear a veil and speak only when spoken to.

She finally sits down on a bench. When I catch up to her, she fingers a button on her sweater, looks down at the ground, and says, "I'm not sure we're going to be able to travel together."

My chest tightens. "I don't understand."

"I just don't think it's going to work. We move at such different speeds. Maybe we should go our separate ways."

I stand up. "You knew how I got around before we left. I don't deserve this." I am surprised not only by my words, but by the force with which I deliver them. "I'm busting my butt to keep up with you, and I'll keep busting my butt. If that isn't good enough, then, fine, we should split up now, because I don't want to hear, I don't deserve to hear, another word about 'different speeds.'" I have no desire to travel alone. I hope she won't call my bluff.

She doesn't. We travel together for the next thirteen weeks. She never says another word about different speeds. I never question her desire for different beds. We visit thirteen countries from Scandinavia to the two Germanys separated by a wall; to the Communist satellites of Hungary, Bulgaria, and Rumania; to Greece, Italy, Switzerland, and, finally, France. I go through two pairs of shoes, three cane tips, and one hundred–plus catheter condoms.

We climb long dirt paths and long stone stairways so that we can see ancient ruins. We climb four flights of stairs to *pensione* rooms without their own toilets so that we can save a couple of dollars a night. Sometimes I can't get all the way to the ruins. Sometimes the bathroom isn't even on the same floor as our room. She never asks me if I mind. I never say I mind. I treat her to numerous dinners, tours, and cultural events. I pay for our transportation. She always says thank you.

In Venice, she takes my hand after a candlelit dinner and a bottle of Chianti. When we return to our *pensione* near the Grand Canal, she kisses me on the lips. My heart begins pounding. Is this the moment I've been waiting for? Then she climbs into her twin bed. "Good night," she says as she rolls over, her back to me. I want to say: "Let me make love to you. It may be awkward, but it will be from the heart." Again, I say nothing.

Kyla's respect for me on the trip is as thick as the callus that develops in the palm of my left hand from leaning on the cane so much, as thick as the callus that develops on my heart when I realize we will not be lovers, as thick as my lack of respect for myself because I never ask her how she feels, never tell her what I want.

In Paris, our last stop, a room-finding service directs us to a hotel near Pigalle. We don't know in advance that this is the city's red-light district, but it doesn't matter. Our lodging is cheap and clean. Only one small bed, but by this time we have spent a few nights in this manner—always chastely, of course.

My Aunt Ruth's Parisian cousins surprised us by knocking on our door early one morning. Their report back to the States about our accommodations has led to years of smirks and winks from Uncle Bud about how Kyla and I must have been on top of each other in that tiny bed in Paris. I have never disabused him of the notion. The illusion that I had fucked my way across Europe with a bright, beautiful woman was my payment for having disappointed myself.

CHAPTER 16

I can't recall the very first question Professor Richard Epstein asked on the very first day of our contracts class at the
University of Chicago Law School in 1973. I can, however, remember the answer given by Ms. Christopher, the unlucky
young woman the professor singled out of the 160 first-year
students in the Class of '76. Actually, nonanswer is more accurate—for when the mortified Ms. Christopher opened her
mouth, no words came out, only an unintelligible stutter that
one might associate with an epileptic seizure or some other
medical catastrophe.

Professor Epstein, not too far removed from his own days
as a student at Yale Law, was gentle. He changed the question
from "essay" to "multiple choice." "Calm down, Ms. Christopher. Can you just give me a yes or a no?"

The stutter had become a death rattle.

"Ms. Christopher, just shake your head yes or no?"

The teacher would have had better luck getting a blink from
a quadriplegic.

As for this quadriplegic, I had been faced with a tough question of my own when walking in a few minutes earlier. One
entered the large lecture hall through either of two doors at

ground level. A desk, a podium, and a blackboard built into the wall indicated that this was the professor's turf, or linoleum. Shallow steps angled up from this level to the back of the room. Each step offered entry to a row of several desks for students—ten rows in all. It made sense that first day that the higher up one sat—the farther away from the professor— the less likely one was to be questioned. Ms. Christopher, for example, had plunked herself down squarely in the professor's sight line, in the center of the third row. Thus, my dilemma: to avoid interrogation, should I select a seat on the back bench, thereby giving myself a demanding climb up several steps—a climb made even harder because the law books in the bag strapped over my shoulder were so heavy? Or should I opt for a more accessible (but visible) desk in one of the lower rows where the air wasn't quite so thin? Remember where Bob Uecker sat in the Miller Lite commercials of the 1980s? That is where I hid myself.

As Ms. Christopher immortalized herself without saying a word (and I buried my head in my book and practiced shaking my head yes, no), a lone hand shot up from the center of the first row—the VIP section. "Yes, Mr. Kaufman."

A voice, at once deep and nasally, offered an answer to the question—in essay fashion.

"That's correct," said Professor Epstein.

I should have guessed that Aaron Kaufman would have been the first in our class not only to supply a correct answer, but to raise his hand. I had met Aaron in the dormitory attached to the law school three days earlier. Professor Epstein had already posted our first assignment. Not since I had made the mistake of taking an upper-level philosophy class in college had I encountered such baffling material. Contract law's theory of "consideration" was as confusing as Kant—and took just as long to read. After one full hour, I had proceeded only eight pages.

Taking a bathroom break, I spied Aaron at his desk. The guy was reading the same heavy, thick red contracts book as I, but he was wearing headphones. Headphones! You'd have to be a genius to be able to get through this material while listening to music. In awe, I knocked on my new neighbor's partially open door. He didn't hear me at first. No doubt because the Led Zeppelin or Doors song blasting in his ears drowned me out. Still, he kept reading.

I knocked again, louder. This time he heard me. He put down his book and stood up. Short and wiry, he could have been a wrestler or a chess club president—probably both, I marveled.

"What can I do for you?" he asked.

I hadn't seen him turn down the headphones which remained on his short, curly brown hair. "I'm amazed you can listen to music and digest this stuff," I shouted. "You—

Aaron held up his hand. "You don't have to yell," he said, taking off the headphones. "Actually, I'm not listening to music. I just wear these to keep out the noise from the hall."

Chess club.

"Oh," I said, comforted that he must also be finding the material impossible to fathom. "Tough going, huh?"

"Not really," he said, sitting down again. "But that may be because I bought the book over the summer and read it before I got here."

The horrors of the first year of law school have been accurately chronicled in movies like *The Paper Chase* and books like Scott Turow's *One L*. As my friends and I struggled over material that seemed as if it were written in a foreign language and, worse, seemed to have absolutely no relevance to the real world, my father intervened.

"You need to see the light at the end of the tunnel," he told me one day after I complained about an assignment I deemed meaningless. He confessed that he had long since lost interest in the Law with a capital *L;* theory held no thrall. But he still loved the lowercase, if not lower-brow, law. He relished the deal-making, the brokering, the thrill of the trial, building a firm, lunching with judges and pols—the practice.

"Sure," I said. "Who wouldn't?" This was the real world that my friends and I missed, wanted to see, and needed to see so that the tunnel we were in promised some light.

And so, a month or two after law school began, my father arranged for me and a half-dozen other classmates to leave our ivory tower and come downtown on a regular basis to experience the real world. One day we spent an afternoon at his firm talking to the lawyers there about their day-to-day work and watching them in action; one week we went to a trial in the courtroom of a state judge whom Dad knew; one week we had lunch in chambers with a distinguished federal judge and sat in on a hearing he was holding. And one week Dad held everyone spellbound with his description of his work for the Colts.

"You're lucky that you'll have such a great place to practice," one of my friends told me.

But my father and I never talked about whether I would join Fiffer & D'Angelo. Entering law school, I had been certain that I wanted to practice elsewhere. I needed to prove to myself and to others that I could succeed on my own, free from my father's assistance and shadow. By the end of the first year, however, I began to have second thoughts. I had grown up enough, was secure enough now, to be able to enjoy his presence without feeling threatened by it. I only felt sorry, almost stupid, that it had taken me so long to conclude that he was my father, not my rival, and that he possessed no hidden agenda to point me in directions he, but not I, desired. Although I still felt I wouldn't want to work with him immediately after law school, I entertained the prospect of joining him someday—after making my own mark—especially if he still represented the Colts.

My law school friends envied my social life as well as my professional prospects. I went out frequently with several women whom I knew from years past. At the same time, I kept in touch with Kyla, who had settled into a government job in Philadelphia. Sharing ups and downs (my ups, her downs) over the telephone, rekindled my feelings for her. When she invited me to join her on a weeklong trip to Puerto Rico before the start of my second year at the law school, I jumped.

My mother advised me not to go. "I love Kyla," she said, "but she's a user."

"I've used her as much as she's used me," I said.

"Two wrongs don't make a right."

But I didn't know how to quit or how to accept failure. I still believed that if you wanted something badly enough and tried your hardest, you'd get it. I wasn't sure why I wanted Kyla—because of who she was or because of who I thought she could make me—but I couldn't turn down this last chance to prove myself.

Kyla had initially explained that she had agreed to go to San Juan with a friend from work and her husband. After I signed on, she told me that Nick, her friend's husband, was blind due to complications from diabetes. He also had only one kidney and required dialysis three days a week. She added that he had failed to come to grips with his condition and remained depressed and quite dependent on his wife.

Rather than complain about this unexpected twist, I found the silver lining: perhaps my independence and positive attitude in the face of this fellow's dependence and negativism would so impress Kyla that she would suddenly beg forgiveness for the way she had treated me in Europe and throw herself upon me.

We had been in San Juan for about an hour when I realized how wrong I was. The four of us were in the swimming pool when Kyla and her friend decided that they wanted to go shopping. Would I mind watching Nick until they returned in an hour or two? They left the two of us in the shallow end, each blind in his own way.

That night I couldn't sleep. Kyla could. I watched her untroubled breathing and finally realized that I would never bridge the arm's length of distance between our two beds.

I blamed that on the accident, of course, on circumstances beyond my control. Had I not been hurt, unable to keep pace with her, unable to assuage any unasked questions she may have had about my sexual ability (and, perhaps, my ability to father children) things would undoubtedly have been different, I reasoned.

Professor Epstein or whoever was teaching domestic relations at the law school would not have been impressed by this display of logic or lack thereof. I imagined an interrogation:

"Mr. Fiffer. Isn't it true that Ms. B. has terminated or avoided relationships with other men who had no physical disabilities?"

"Yes."

"Isn't it true that you, yourself, have terminated or avoided relationships with other women who have no physical disabilities?"

"Yes."

"Indeed, since the beginning of recorded history, haven't millions of men and women terminated or avoided relationships for reasons that had nothing to do with physical disability?"

"Yes."

"Yet you are convinced that the sole reason Ms. B. does not wish to have a relationship with you, to *marry you,* is because of your disability?"

"Yes."

"There can't be any other reason?"

"None that I can figure."

"You're perfect other than the way you walk?"

Typical professor's trick, putting words into my mouth.

"While you're thinking, let me ask you this, Mr. Fiffer: is your entire image of yourself based on your disability?"

"Not entire, but—"

"And you assume that because it is so important to you, it is important to everyone else—or at least the women you date?"

Silence.

"Mr. Fiffer, just answer yes or no. Just shake your head."

I'm not tongue-tied. Most law students feel the need to answer immediately lest their silence be interpreted as ignorance, and the professor moves on, often after embarrassing us. I need time to think about this.

Okay. "I understand what you're getting at, Professor. I could say that love knows no logic, but that would be disingenuous. It's entirely possible that Kyla and others who have rejected me and those that will no doubt reject me in the future will do so for reasons completely unrelated to my disability. Kyla has seen me act like a jerk enough times to write me off for that alone. Maybe my stupid Fiffer Code scares her rather than attracts her.

"I realize that since I've never had the courage to discuss my disability with her or other women that I have no right to put words into their mouths, ascribe my reasoning to theirs. All I can say is that my disability and I are inseparable. It impacts everything I do—even more, I would argue, than, say, one's skin color or religion. I cannot take a step without being aware of it—whether in public or by myself. Keeping my balance is a full-time job. I am the air traffic controller processing, in a split second, information coming at me from all sides, to avoid a collision. I am the Secret Service bodyguard scanning the crowd, the room, for anything out of the ordinary. I am the advance man figuring out all the logistics. Are there stairs? Is there a railing? Where's the bathroom?

"I live with myself every day, and if it affects my every move, I can't imagine it not affecting others around me."

CHAPTER 17

The phone call came on Friday the thirteenth. It was my mother. "Hang on," I said. "Let me grab a chair." I had just walked in the door to my apartment a few blocks away from the law school. I had taken my last exam of the quarter earlier in the day and then rushed to the Y for Dick's one o'clock workout.

My class schedule during my second year of law school forced me to rush every day. Traffic on Lake Shore Drive from Hyde Park to the Near North Side was often heavy, and I was frequently late. Dick cut me less slack for tardiness than my law school professors. "This is the fourth time this month, Crip. Go back to the ivory tower," he had said a week earlier when I walked in three minutes after the workout started. Everyone was on the floor doing leg raises.

"Sorry." I sat on the bench and prepared to lower myself to the mat.

Dick held up his hand and signaled "stop" to me. "I mean it. Go home," he said. "You don't need this. You're in perfect shape. Go back and play with your pansy friends at that pansy school that doesn't even have a football team."

He was wrong on several counts. The University of Chicago did have a football team. My friends weren't pansies. And I wasn't in perfect shape. I was still on the cane and needed the workout.

As my mother waited on the phone, I put down Dick's latest incentive—a gym bag lettered "Woit's Warriors"—and grabbed a chair. "What's up?" I finally asked.

"How did your finals go?"

"Fine."

"Are you still planning on coming home tomorrow?" she asked.

"Tomorrow or Sunday."

"Well," she said matter-of-factly, "your dad's in the hospital."

"Hospital? Why? Is he okay?" I suddenly felt light-headed.

"He seems to be. He's been having chest pains on and off the last few days, so Dr. Elisberg thought it would be a good idea—"

I cut her off. "He hasn't had a heart attack?"

"Oh no," my mother said. She still sounded matter-of-fact. "This is just what they call 'for observation.'"

"I think I'll come home tonight," I said.

I knew that my father was to have flown to Minneapolis earlier in the day for a business meeting with the legendary former Baltimore Colts quarterback Johnny Unitas. Those chest pains must have been pretty serious to prevent him from going. He had always admired Johnny U. and had looked forward to sitting down with him since becoming the Colts' lawyer. This was one more perk of having such a great client. In addition to working on team business, Dad accompanied the Chicago-based Bob Irsay to several games a year as well as the Super Bowl, no matter who was playing. Mom always went with him to the Super Bowl, and Jim and Tommy and I went to at least one game a year in Baltimore. There, we'd

lunch in the Stadium Club on oysters and crab cakes while trying not to gawk at heroes from our childhood like Lenny
Moore, Raymond Berry, and Art Donovan.

.   .   .

I had been in Highland Park Hospital only once since my release in April 1968. Entering the main entrance on my way to
see a friend in 1972, I had immediately felt dizzy—a state of
affairs I chose to blame on the high-powered chemicals used to
disinfect the hospital rather than the high-powered memories
of the event that had brought me there. Now as I headed toward the Cardiac Care Unit, I ascribed my dizziness to ner-
vousness about my father's condition. I had always feared that
he would drop dead from a heart attack.

This unit was just around the corner from the Intensive
Care Unit where I had spent my first nights after my accident
seven years earlier. I didn't pass out when I saw Dad (as he
had when he had first seen me), but my legs felt shaky. He
was flat on his back in the hospital bed and looked pale and
frightened in an ill-fitting hospital gown. I wasn't used to
seeing him in a position where he wasn't in control, wasn't
confident. Wires emanated from his chest and his wrist. "I'm
hooked to a monitor," he explained. "If I have another one
of these spasms in my chest, it will register at the nurse's station."

He had suffered one minor spasm since he'd arrived, but
wouldn't have another until the following afternoon. I was
there. His brother had just come into the unit. My father and
my Uncle Bill were not estranged, but even though they lived
within fifteen minutes of each other, they rarely socialized or
spoke. The story went that Bill, a sales rep for Sears, was jeal-

ous of Dad's success. Who knew? And who knew whether Bill's visit caused or merely coincided with the spasm.

Uncle Bill had not even reached the bed when Dad put his hand to his chest. His eyes widened for a few seconds and then returned to their normal size. "Whoa, that was a doozy," he said. "Biggest one yet." A nurse quickly confirmed his assessment. She entered purposefully, but not to cause alarm. "Are you all right, Mr. Fiffer?" she asked.

Dad's internist, Eddie Elisberg, responded to the doozy spasm by calling in one of Chicago's leading cardiologists, who immediately ordered Dad transferred to Northwestern Memorial Hospital in the city. There, an angiogram revealed no arterial blockage. The cardiologist's message: You are overweight, you smoke, you don't exercise, you are stressed out, but you've got time to save yourself. Change your lifestyle now, and you'll be fine. The doctor added that my mother should stop smoking, too. After years as a three-pack-a-day user, she quit that evening and has never picked up a cigarette since.

Dad left the hospital two days later and proceeded to do everything the doctor ordered. He put away his cigarettes; he gave up hard liquor; he went on a diet; he started walking and swimming regularly. He talked about cutting back his hours at work. He knew that while the firm was his greatest source of fulfillment, it was also his greatest source of stress. His partner, Dino D'Angelo, remained institutionalized, but Dad had kept his friend on the payroll for several years. Now, the younger partners, angry that firm profits due them were being unjustly diverted to someone who wasn't contributing, were applying pressure to cut Dino loose. At the same time, another partner was applying pressure on Dad to keep up the payments. Dad had initiated discussions to reach a lump-sum settlement to buy Dino out. But no one could agree on the size of the lump.

Jim came home for Christmas vacation just as Dad came home from the hospital. The two of us drove down to his office to pick up some papers he needed. Fiffer & D'Angelo occupied the top floor of the Rookery, a landmark building designed by the famed Chicago architects Burnham & Root. The small, cherry-wood–paneled waiting room featured three expensive leather chairs and a matching couch. "It talks money," Dad had once said. "When a client walks in, he knows to expect a big bill." The waiting room and interior halls were adorned with paintings, most of which had been acquired by Dino before his illness. Much of the artwork was modern, but the prize possession was Norman Rockwell's portrait of John F. Kennedy.

Dad's corner office was as large as the combination dining room/living room space in my apartment and better furnished—with its own leather couch, an antique mahogany credenza, and a small conference table and chairs. His large rectangular desk featured several family pictures, including one of himself and his father outside the hamburger grill. It felt eerie being here without him. We found what he wanted and hurried out.

I stayed at home rather than at my apartment for much of the winter break. I watched as Dad took brisk walks each morning, went swimming on the weekends, and tried to relax by spending more time at his hobbies. He organized and reorganized his classical tapes and wine bottles. He read and reread travel brochures and magazines. He ordered a variety of bushes and annuals for spring planting.

THREE QUARTERS, TWO DIMES, AND A NICKEL 233

Family friends came for dinner on New Year's Eve. "Why don't you give up the practice and take a judgeship?" a fellow lawyer asked. "Much less pressure."

"I've thought about that," Dad said. His voice was flat, his eyes sad. "I'd miss the action."

The following week, Dad went back to work part-time. He was feeling better. The doctor had given him nitroglycerin tablets to be used whenever he felt a spasm. He had taken only two or three since leaving the hospital. Still, I worried. After school resumed in January, I came home almost every weekend. I usually brought a classmate or two for dinner.

On a Saturday night early in February, my father and I again talked about the pros and cons of taking a judgeship. Two friends had accompanied me, and Dad was most interested in where they would be working when school ended in June. He had already hired two of my childhood pals who were graduating in the spring, and he had one clerkship remaining for a second-year student.

I had already made up my mind that I didn't want the position—not that he had offered it to me. I had committed to a summer job with Wildman, Harrold, Allen & Dixon, a Chicago firm that was twice as big as Fiffer & D'Angelo. "I can't see you as anything but a trial lawyer," Dad had said earlier in the fall when I had confessed that corporate law, tax law, securities work, and estate planning did not appeal to me and that I was beginning to have doubts about practicing law. "Take a clerkship at a firm that does trial work and then take the class in trial practice before you make up your mind."

This made sense. I might not be that great standing on my feet, but I felt comfortable thinking on my feet. I relished competition, and since sports were out, maybe I could get my thrills in combat by trial. Trial-practice participants prepared a case and then presented it before a mock jury. I made a mental note to sign up for it the following fall, because it was open only to third-year students. Then I interviewed with firms that specialized in litigation.

Wildman, Harrold seemed like the right place for several reasons in addition to this specialization. It had been created only a few years earlier by highly respected lawyers dissatisfied with their lots at one of the city's oldest, largest, and most prestigious firms. Unhappy with that firm's stodginess and lack of regard for its own trial lawyers, they had left to create an environment that encouraged individuality and moved young lawyers into the courtroom faster than any other practice in the city. The partners and associates were brash, bright, hungry, and multidimensional. I was particularly impressed that the fellow that interviewed me appeared to know the recording artist of every song written since Elvis Presley's debut twenty years earlier.

One of the friends whom I had brought home for dinner on that night in February would be working for a big firm in New York, the other in a large Boston firm. I remember that we sat around the dinner table for a long time talking with Dad about our upcoming jobs. I remember that the dinner included a vegetable I had never heard of—fennel. I remember that Mom had sent out the cushions on the family room couch and chairs for reupholstering and that when we finally moved from the dinner table, Dad sat on the cushionless couch, an uncomfortable prisoner of circumstances beyond his control. I remember that as we said our good-nights, Dad turned on the television; Alfred Hitchcock's *Frenzy* was on. I remember that on the ride back to Hyde Park I wondered, as I did each time I left home, if I would ever see my father alive again. I remember thinking that our relationship had never been better and that I didn't want him to die. I remember thinking about a television show I had watched earlier in the week about the author John Gunther and his son, who had died an early death. I had cried at the end of the movie and had thought about picking up the phone to tell Dad that I loved him. I hadn't.

The morning after our dinner, my father and my Uncle Bud went for their regular Sunday morning swim at the Hilton Hotel. After doing his laps for half an hour, Dad returned home. He had lunch, and then he and my mother and my brother Tommy headed for my aunt and uncle's house in Highland Park. Bud and Ruth had invited them and about twenty other friends and neighbors to see vacation films.

Ten minutes into the ride, just a few blocks from their destination, Dad pulled the car to the side of the road.

"What's wrong?" asked my mother.

My father took out a nitroglycerin tablet. "A spasm. Another doozy." He placed the tablet in his mouth.

"Do you want to go to the hospital?"

They were about ten minutes away from Highland Park Hospital.

"No. Eddie will be at the party." Dad's internist was among those invited to see the travelogue.

My father directed the car back onto the road. A minute later, he pulled into my aunt and uncle's driveway. He put the car into "park" and turned off the ignition. Then he slumped over the steering wheel.

"Bob!" my mother cried.

No answer. She told Tommy to run to the house and get Bud.

No other guests had arrived yet. Bud hurried out, while Ruth called the paramedics. They were there quickly, pulling into the driveway just as the guests began arriving on foot and by car. They pulled my father off the steering wheel, laid him on the frigid asphalt and began CPR. They gave him oxygen. They defibrillated him. My mother watched in horror along with several of my aunt and uncle's neighbors whom she barely knew.

.   .   .

I was in my apartment watching a basketball game on television when my aunt called. "Your father had a heart attack," she said.

"Is he alive?"

"I don't know. They took him to the hospital."

"Where should I go?"

"Come here first."

I hadn't planned on going out this cold Sunday afternoon. I didn't even have my leg bag on. I hooked it up, put on my Baltimore Colts warm-up jacket for good luck, and took off.

"Please be alive. Please be alive. Please be alive." I repeated the mantra for the forty-five minutes that it took to get to Bud and Ruth's.

I parked the Malibu that my father had bought me and taught me to drive. I was halfway up the walk when my mother came out of the house. A bad sign, I thought. Why isn't she at the hospital?

She put her left arm in my free right one. "We didn't make it this time," she said.

I choose to think that my father saved the lives of my mother and brother by hanging on until he was in Bud and Ruth's driveway and had stopped the car. If he had slumped over the steering wheel any earlier, they all might have crashed into oncoming traffic, a tree, or one of the houses lining the road.

That night, we received our closest friends at my aunt and uncle's house. I kept my Colts jacket on the entire evening. Tommy sat in a corner reading *The Count of Monte Cristo*.

Before going home, we picked up my brother Jim at the airport. Because he was eight hundred miles away in New Haven or because he chose not to think about it, Jim had not contemplated Dad's death. He and my father had been going through the on-again, off-again romance typical of college seniors and their parents—the same romance I had gone through four years earlier. When he got into the car, Jim burst into tears and melted into my mother's arms. "Did he know how much I loved him?"

I still hadn't cried.

The next morning, we went to the funeral home to pick out a casket. In the afternoon, the rabbi came to our house. We shared our thoughts about my father so that the rabbi could prepare the eulogy for the next day's funeral. "He was like the Godfather," I remember saying. "If anybody had a problem, needed something, he took care of it." Later in the day, one of those people Dad had helped called from Philadelphia. "I wish I could put my arms around you right now," Kyla said. She hoped I would understand that flying to the funeral was just too expensive. I didn't.

That night friends and clients filled the house. When Robert Irsay, the owner of the Colts, marched in, the law firm partners abandoned us to make sure his every need was

met. He was my father's client and now that my father was
gone, there was some question about the firm's ability to retain his business as well as the business of others essential for
the financial well-being and continued operation of Fiffer &
D'Angelo.

Later that evening, my dad's accountant, a man more adept
with numbers than with people, told me, "You know, your
dad never recovered from your accident. I think in the long
run that's what killed him." I had never considered the toll my
accident may have taken on my father. I held back the tears
and my impulse to punch the bean counter in the face.

In the shower the next morning, I fell apart. I wasn't crying because I was frightened about the future. I knew we Fiffers would survive. Mom's strength, so evident when I had
been hurt, was again manifesting itself. She hadn't wavered
in public, had even comforted others by telling them how
special they had been to Dad. She would hold herself together, as well as the family. Still, I cried for her, widowed at
fifty with a son not yet ten. Tommy would be well cared for
by a remarkable mother, by Jim and me, and by countless
friends of the family. Still, I cried for my little brother, who
would never have the opportunity to learn from my father as
we had. Jim had had that opportunity and used it to good
advantage. Still, I cried for him because his long-positive relationship with Dad had been in limbo and he would have to
conquer guilt and anger as well as sadness. I cried for Dad,
of course. The clichés were true: He had packed much more
into his forty-eight years than most men and women, and he
had accomplished more than most do in a lifetime—but he
was so young. He would never have the chance to build the
firm even bigger, watch his friends gain higher political of-

fice, and, therefore, gain even greater political power himself. More important, he would never have the chance to fully enjoy the fruits of his labor with his sounding board and confidante, Mom. He would never plant the garden he had planned, hear all the symphonies he had taped, drink all the wine, see the world, enjoy his children as adults and, perhaps, even law partners. He would never know our wives or children, his grandchildren.

Finally, I cried for myself. I was luckier than Tommy; I'd had a father for almost twenty-five years. I was more fortunate than Jim; in the eighteen months since I had returned to Chicago for law school, I had matured enough to stop competing with Dad, to stop ootzing. I had allowed myself the pleasure of being his son and allowed him the pleasure of being my father. Too little, too late.

The funeral, held in a large chapel, was standing room only. Prominent politicians, judges, newspapermen, attorneys, and businessmen attended. The dean of the law school came (because he was my father's friend, not mine). Neighbors, friends, many of my classmates, and others whom the Godfather had helped also attended. "You'll have to remind me who some of your friends are," my mother whispered to me as we took our seats in the first row of the chapel, a few feet from the flower-covered casket that held my father. I sat to her left so that those coming up to offer condolences would have to pass me first. Tommy sat to her right, gripping her arm. Jim sat to Tommy's right. My father's eighty-year-old mother, heavily tranquilized, sat beside Jim. Uncle Bud and Aunt Ruth filled out our row.

I do not recall anything the rabbi said in his eulogy. I do remember that when the funeral was over our family was to exit via a side door before anyone else in attendance left. I made sure that Tommy, Jim, and my mother exited ahead of me. Bud signaled for me to precede him. I motioned for him to go first. He did. I wanted everyone who was watching to know that I was taking responsibility for the family now.

CHAPTER 18

Had my father lived to the age of fifty, he would have seen me graduate at the head of the class from the law school he loved so much.

Our graduation ceremony took place on a warm, sunny June afternoon in Rockefeller Chapel, a huge Gothic edifice just north of the famous Midway. Law school officials herded the 150-odd graduates-to-be in the Class of 1976 into a large room in the chapel's cavernous basement. There, black-gowned and mortar-boarded, we lined up in alphabetical order, Mr. Adams to Ms. Zelinsky. On cue Mr. Adams et al. snaked to a stairway leading up to ground level. On cue again, Mr. Adams moved with deliberate haste up the stairs. Ms. Agnew followed his precedent, then Mr. Allen and Mr. Atherton. Our marching orders called for us to exit a side door to the outside, then loop around quickly to the large doors at the back of the chapel—a twenty-five- or thirty-yard trek. As the chapel's mighty organ played Bach and Beethoven, we would then join a processional led by the university president, the law school dean, and various other dignitaries bearing maces, scepters, and flags.

There was just one problem: I knew there was no way I would be able to keep up with the twenty or so classmates ahead of me as they climbed the stairs and continued on the outside route. That meant that the 130 classmates behind me wouldn't be able to keep up either. As I watched those at the front of the line start moving, I remembered *The Great Escape*, a terrific movie based on the true story of an Allied breakout from a World War II stalag. On the night of the long-awaited escape, POW Cavendish tripped on his suitcase while climbing out of the tunnel, thus alerting the Germans to the scheme. As a result, the one hundred-plus men behind him never made it to the top. It might be argued that they were lucky, as the Nazis rounded up all but three of the seventy who preceded them and shot fifty of the would-be escapees to death. In my case, however, being the Cavendish who denied those behind me the chance to receive their diplomas in timely fashion was, to use a law school term, *distinguishable* from the Great Escape; unless the Nazis were waiting for us at the top of the stairs, I wasn't doing any of my classmates a hidden service by delaying them.

What to do? I suppose I could have stood aside, let everyone pass me on the stairs, and then straggled in (out of order) at the end of the line. That was the selfless gesture, but I wasn't feeling selfless. No, this demanded a bold, adventuresome, clever, selfish plan of action—finding a shortcut.

When I reached the top of the stairs, the others in the conga line still dutifully behind me in alphabetical order, I scanned the grounds with the special shortcut-finding sensor that had miraculously appeared when I had become ambulatory again after the accident. Aha! My sensor spied a middle-aged woman in a tasteful floral print leaning against an open door less than ten yards away. She was fanning herself with what appeared to be a program. Could she have sought to escape the oppressive heat in the chapel by finding a portal on the main-floor level? Yes, I discovered after hurriedly leading my charges in her direction. And the path from this side door to the main aisle was clear and wide.

The procession is already moving down that aisle. University President Gray, Law School Dean Casper, regents unknown. But none of my classmates.

I take my group in the side door, as if that had been the plan from the beginning. Reaching the intersection of this side aisle and the main one, I stop. Adams through Fields have still not arrived. Who would have thought that I'd ever stand first in my class? I smile, confident that I will always be able to find a way to get to where I want to go.

.   .   .

I knew where I wanted to go after having a postceremony dinner with my family. I phoned Nan, the attractive schoolteacher I'd been dating for a couple of months. We had met on campus at a lecture by Watergate reporter Bob Woodward.

"Funny you should call," her roommate told me. "As we speak, Nan is writing 'Mrs. Steve Fiffer' on a pad of paper over and over." I heard giggling in the background. "Well, you are," the roommate said to Nan.

I wasn't surprised. I was beginning to picture her as my wife. I envisioned our life together: I would practice law at Wildman, Harrold, where I had accepted a full-time job. (Sadly, my father's firm had dissolved after his death.) Nan would continue to teach until we had children. I'd gradually get involved in politics—either through family friend Mike Howlett, who was running for governor, or through the office of Mayor Daley, which was considering me for a position as adviser on matters related to the aging and the disabled. We would live in the city at first, but move to the suburbs—maybe even Glencoe—when we had kids. I'd take them to Wrigley Field and Comiskey Park and maybe take a trip east some day, say to Yankee Stadium. It sounded familiar—and wonderful.

I would continue to work out with Dick. Not because I expected to get off the cane. I was resigned to the possibility that I would need it for the foreseeable future, probably until science provided a cure. I could live with this, however—because I was independent and because I had Nan. I now had a different reason for continuing with Coach: I wanted to remain in good health and live well beyond forty-eight.

Nan and I enjoyed a romantic summer. We celebrated the Fourth of July, my birthday a week later (she gave me a pan for making crepes), and the conclusion of the bar exam at the end of the month. Then without warning, she became distant, unavailable. A few weeks after that my mother summoned me to the house. "I ran into Betty Wolfe yesterday," she said ominously. "She's friends with Nan's mother."

Betty had told Nan's mom how happy she was that we were together. The feeling was not mutual. "We don't need Fiffer's troubles," Nan's mother replied.

I hadn't seen it coming. I had finally stopped attributing every failed romance to my physical condition, or "troubles." I had watched the relationships of friends who weren't on canes or crutches fall apart for a myriad of reasons. I had broken up with girls for reasons that had nothing to do with appearance.

When my mother told me what Nan's mother had said, I thought back to the woman from Manhattanville—and my silence. Then I thought back to Kyla—and my silence. Then I drove straight to Nan's building, climbed up to her second-floor apartment on my cane, and confronted her.

It didn't take a lawyer to extract a confession. Nan admitted that her parents had sat her down and told her all the reasons why she should stop seeing me. They had compiled a laundry list of things they thought I couldn't do, reminding her how much she liked to travel, how much she liked to play tennis, how badly she wanted to have a family. Her father, a doctor, had recited a host of spinal cord injury–related medical complications that might materialize in future years.

I did not go gentle into the night. As she sat crying, I reminded her that I had traveled across Europe under the most trying physical circumstances. I acknowledged that I couldn't play tennis with her, but suggested that many spouses didn't play sports together and that I would be happy to help find her a tennis partner, a search that didn't seem terribly difficult. I said that nobody had ever told me that I couldn't have children. As for future medical complications, I told her that because I worked out five days a week with Dick Woit, I felt like I was in pretty good shape. I admitted that I couldn't predict the future, but then again neither could any guy she met. Indeed, I said, she couldn't guarantee that she would always be healthy and fit, but I was willing to take the chance.

I told her, "With me, what you see is what you get." Everybody has problems, I said; mine are just more visible than those of other people. I said that I thought my emotional strength was more important than the strength of my backhand.

She said she'd think things over, but I knew that we would never get back together. "You may not be getting a dollar bill, but you'd be getting three quarters, two dimes, and a nickel," I said on the way out. "I may be different, but I'm whole." It was the first time that I had publicly acknowledged that I was different. After I said it, instead of feeling weak as I had always feared, I felt remarkably strong.

CHAPTER 19

"Who the hell are you?" Dick asks.

"I'm Steve's—"

"You Sherry? Jeez, you got a big ass."

She hates being called Sherry.

"Jeez, I thought Stevie could do better than you."

She keeps opening her mouth, but no words come out.

"How old are you?"

"I'm . . ."

Her name is Sharon, not Sherry. She is thirty-one, the same age I am. And, having known her for almost a year and dated her for the last five months, I'm certain I *can't* do any better.

I met her in August of 1981, a few years and a few women after Nan. On the way to an outdoor concert, I had stopped with a date at a large party at the Evanston home of my old friend Rensy, whom everyone now called "Rens." I spotted Sharon across the backyard deck as I grabbed a couple of beers from a cooler by the back door. She was pretty—dark brown hair down to her shoulders, deep brown eyes, a long, thin neck to die for—but I was drawn to her that first evening by her smile—a smile that was not directed at me, but at a bubbly little blond girl of about four, swinging from an old tire tied to the branch of a tree. I had no idea what the relationship was between this woman and child, but the woman's broad smile was one of joy and wonder—a smile that made me want to meet her.

Rens, who was now an internist at Cook County Hospital (and on his way to becoming one of the country's leading authorities on AIDS), introduced us a few minutes later, noting only that Sharon lived across the street and belonged to Kate, the girl on the swing. We exchanged hellos and then caught ourselves looking over at each other several times before my date and I left. I talked to Rens a few days later and asked him about Sharon, but several months would pass before our first date.

I had left Wildman, Harrold by the time of that first meeting. While in law school, I had begun to do some freelance writing for magazines and newspapers. I had continued during my first two years at the firm.

My articles were hardly weighty. Typical was a piece for the *Chicago Tribune Magazine* on the eighteen greatest miniature golf holes in the area. Initially, I was satisfied just to receive a byline and enjoy the fun of stringing words together. But after a while, I yearned to write articles of greater substance. There wasn't time, however. I was too busy at the law firm, where I had an interesting workload of cases in various stages of litigation and was getting excellent training as a trial lawyer.

When I told a writer friend, Ira Berkow, of my dilemma, he suggested I ask the firm for a leave of absence to write and sort out career possibilities. Firm founder Max Wildman graciously granted the leave, promising to keep me on the letterhead and pay my insurance until I made up my mind. Eighteen months later my brother Jim graduated from the University of Chicago Law School and decided that he wanted to join Wildman, Harrold. Max reminded me that the firm had a nepotism rule; only one family member could practice there at a time. By this time, I had moved on to more serious writing projects and had decided that I preferred this over practicing law. My shingle came down and Jim's went up. I was completing work on a documentary film about disabled athletes when I met Sharon.

Rens told me that Sharon held a theater degree from the University of Illinois, where she had performed improv, acted, and directed with some success. After a long break, she had gone back to school and was now earning a masters in English and creative writing at the University of Illinois–Chicago. She had grown up Catholic in Kankakee, a river town sixty miles south of Chicago. Her parents had owned a tavern there called the E-Z Way Inn. She was, he said, a single parent, a widow.

I ran into mother and daughter a few more times at Rens's house over the next months. I was still seeing someone else, but I found Sharon immensely attractive. She was devoted to Kate, an open and engaging kid who was already reading. She had a wonderful sense of humor—we relished the same shows, *SCTV* and *Fawlty Towers*—and she was as conversant and interested in pop culture as she was in English literature. She was the only person I knew who could expound on both Bart Maverick and Roland Barthes. She didn't play tennis, didn't smoke, and let it be known that she would never give a crepe pan to a boyfriend for his birthday. "Where's the romance in that?" she asked.

Most important, she had a quality of inner strength that I had observed in only one other person—my mother. She had already gone through about as much as Mom had, too. One unusually warm October night while we sat together on Rens's deck, she told me her story. Seven years earlier, she had broken up with a longtime boyfriend, Gene, quit her job as a fashion writer for Marshall Field's in Chicago, and moved to Minneapolis. Gene had called her a few months later. He told her that he had just been diagnosed with the debilitating and fatal ALS, Lou Gehrig's disease.

Certain that his parents lacked both the financial and emotional means to care for him and that he would eventually end up in a nursing home, Sharon informed Gene that she was returning to Chicago, that they were going to marry, and that she was going to be with him for better or worse. Only a handful of friends at the wedding knew the terrible secret. After the ceremony, Sharon and Gene took off in an old van and crisscrossed the country for almost a year. He was in a wheelchair before too long, and she lugged him everywhere. When his worsening condition made travel impossible, they settled in a cabin in Petersburg, Illinois, a small town outside Springfield.

To their great surprise, Sharon became pregnant. She gave birth to Kate in June of 1977. Gene grew increasingly weak and dependent. He could barely move or talk. He died at age twenty-eight, ten months after Kate was born.

Sharon and I began dating about six months after our first meeting. She invited me to a Christmas party at her apartment, and then a few weeks later I asked her to dinner (at an accessible restaurant). I made sure that Jim and his wife Linda came along so that I'd make a good impression; I was at my best conversation- and humor-wise when playing off my brother.

Sharon asked me out on our next date. We went to see Chicago's professional indoor soccer team, the Sting, play at the Chicago Stadium. This time she brought along a married couple with whom she felt comfortable. I approached the evening with a certain hesitancy. Some seats at the Stadium were hard for me to get to. I liked to know in advance exactly where I would be sitting. I also liked to have someone like Jim or Bill Solomon alongside, someone who knew when to offer assistance and how to help me. I'd feel uncomfortable asking Sharon or her friends to lend an arm or shoulder to lean on.

As Sharon and I entered the stadium, a large, middle-aged woman wearing a pink T-shirt came over to us. "Our group is over there," she said to me. She pointed to a nearby section populated by several pink-shirted people in wheelchairs. I thought they might be patients on an outing from the Rehab Institute. "I'm not with them," I bristled and brushed right past her. As I continued to our real seats, I worried if I'd sounded too harsh. I had nothing against the people in the wheelchairs; I just didn't want to be lumped into a category with them—especially when I was trying to impress my date (as I tried to impress all dates) with my "normalcy."

I quickly learned, however, that Sharon was one woman who could look beyond my body. That made her special and, of course, appealed to me. But, strangely, at the same time, her own history, her blindness to disability, gave me pause. Is something wrong with her? I wondered. Is she only attracted to "wounded heroes"—men who have fallen ill or been injured? In a strange variation on the old Groucho Marx line about not wanting to join any club that would accept him as a member, I wondered whether I should want any woman who would so readily look beyond the cane and accept me. I was so accustomed to the challenge of having to prove myself with women (whether I really had to or I just imagined I had to) that this seemed too easy—even though the one thing I wanted more than anything else in the world was to have the right woman love me. And Sharon was the right woman.

A year or so before we met, I had shed my leg bag and with it any lingering inhibitions of sexual intimacy. When Kate saw me at the breakfast table the morning after my first night with Sharon, she seemed happy to have the company. I was just as happy to be passing the toast to someone so cute and precocious.

I had never imagined myself becoming a father at the same time I became a husband. I had always envisioned myself as a lawyer. I had thought I'd move back to Glencoe. For all my talk about wanting to be independent, I had aspired to my father's life. I realized now I wanted and was living my own life.

By the beginning of the summer, I am convinced that Sharon and Kate are the girls for me. So is my mother, who keeps telling me how different and superior Sharon is to all the girls I had previously dated. There remains one final five-foot-seven-inch, 130-pound hurdle, however.

I haven't thrown Sharon into the lion's den without fair warning. I have described Dick Woit to her hundreds of times, but she is still unprepared for the leprechaun who greets her by telling her she has a big ass.

Dick stands by the entrance to a clean, well-lit room with bright white walls and new oak exercise benches. He has recently moved from the YMCA to a popular health club in Chicago's Lincoln Park area, and he has admitted women to his cult. As he interrogates Sharon, several women of varying shapes, sizes, and ages enter the room and sit on the mat. One woman in her sixties, dignified and regal, wears matching sweats. Another coiffed, heavily made-up woman flashes her long red nails at Dick and interrupts, "Dick dear, where should I go for ribs tonight?"

Dick rolls his eyes and barks: "How the fuck should I know?"

Two more women Sharon's age, mismatched clothes, no makeup, come in and take their spots on the mats.

Dick walks to his spot, sits, and starts the class.

"Just follow me, Sherry," he says almost gently.

Sharon nods, reaching for her toes, listening to Dick count.

"And don't do what that fat ass does," Dick barks, gesturing to the ribs eater. "She's a cheater."

"Oh, Dick, I don't cheat and you know—"

"Shut up."

Sharon is already fading in the first round of leg lifts. The woman next to her whispers, "Just try, just don't put your legs down."

"Stop telling her how to cheat. This is Stevie's girlfriend. You know Stevie, right? Harriet, you know Stevie? The cripple in Paul's class?"

"Yes, Dick. I know Stevie," Harriet, the dignified older woman says. She smiles at Sharon.

"You know, Sherry, Stevie came in here and he couldn't even blink his eyes," Dick says. "He tell you that? He tell you how I saved him? He was nothing, a worthless piece of shit, but I got him on his feet." Dick half closes his eyes in reverie. "Yeah, he couldn't do nothing. But he didn't give up. I'll give him that."

They start doing sit-ups. By her count, they're at 2,004.

"How old's your kid?" Dick asks.

"Five."

"Yeah. Girl?"

"Yes."

"Yeah, well you won't live to see her make thirteen."

"Dick!" Harriet is old enough and obviously secure enough to exercise some authority of her own.

"Yeah, well, I'm just telling the truth. Look at you, Sherry, you're pathetic. You can't breathe. You can't hold your legs up. You look like you're going to have a stroke when you do your sit-ups."

Dick looks over at Harriet. "It's the truth, she's gonna die if she don't get in shape."

Sharon can't help it. She starts to laugh.

"What the fuck you laughing at? It's the truth."

Sharon is delirious by now. She nods. "I know."

Dick's smiling now, too. "Stevie's got trouble. You got a big can and you're an idiot."

She's into the rhythm of the insults, if not the leg lifts.

She's in so much pain that she has detached her body from her head. She can float, too. She doesn't think she'll be able to leave the mat. Dick comes over and lies down next to her. She knows trouble is ahead.

"You ever do a push-up?"

"I think so."

"Yeah, you don't push yourself away from food on the table too often though, do you?"

Dick shows her how to put her feet up on the bench against the wall and get up on her arms. "Do as many as you can with us, don't go down, just stay up on your arms."

She manages to stay up during the push-ups. "Dick staring at me, muttering about my funeral helped," she later said, adding that she found it fascinating to watch her arms go rigid, then numb, then begin to shake. "I actually distanced myself enough to wonder exactly when they would snap like twigs," she said.

After the push-ups, everyone but Harriet gets up to go outside for wind sprints out in the street. Sharon runs them in a fog. Through the haze, she sees a limousine pull up. She wonders if it might be the hearse Dick ordered for her. No, it's just Harriet's limo. The older woman gets in and waves goodbye.

"Oh God, take me with you. Please, take me with you,"

Sharon wants to say, but instead, she turns to follow Dick back into the club.

"So, do you think I should come back?" She's breathing again, but limping.

"I think you better. You're gonna die pretty soon if you don't get in shape."

She tells him she'll see him tomorrow.

"Stevie's a good guy. Did I tell you he couldn't blink his eyes when he came in here?"

She feels every muscle in her "piece of shit, fat-ass body" screaming in pain and realizes that by tomorrow she will only be able to blink her eyes.

She blinks once for "yes."

Dick nods. "Yeah, tell Stevie you did okay."

She smiles.

"Tell him I thought he coulda done better than you, though." He pats her on the shoulder and she is dismissed.

She drags herself up the stairs to my apartment, where Kate and I are playing an Uncle Piggily board game. She limps past us into the master bedroom and collapses on the bed without saying a word. Kate and I bring her dinner in bed, but she is already sound asleep.

"She's gotta lose some weight, and she can't do shit in the workout," Dick tells me the next day, "but I like her. You did good, Stevie. Your girl's got balls."

.   .   .

Later that summer, after telling Dick we were taking a week off from our respective workouts, we drove my brother Tom to New Haven for the start of his freshman year at Yale. I proposed to Sharon in a Holiday Inn a few blocks from my old room at Timothy Dwight College. "How many times have you done that in this motel?" she laughed.

We set the wedding for June 1983. A few days before the ceremony, my brothers hosted a stag party for me at Comiskey Park. Walking to the parking lot after the game, I did not have to hold on to Jim. I was well aware, however, that whenever we moved through such crowded venues—ballparks, movie theaters, busy sidewalks—Jim assumed the role of my body-guard. Silently, so as not to make me feel dependent, he watched for running children, older people not paying atten-tion, drunken fans—anyone who might bump into me and send me to the ground. If he did sense danger, he nonchalantly stationed himself behind me or at my side.

A few years earlier, on a cold April day on the other side of the city, we had exited Wrigley Field and were walking down Addison Street among several thousand Cubs fans. I had felt Jim move from my flank to my rear, and then I lost him. I turned around. Several yards back, he had his hand on the throat of a kid of about twenty whom he had pinned against the side of a charter bus parked near the ballpark. He thrust the kid's head against the side of the bus, then let him go.

"What was that about?" I had asked when he caught up to me.

"He was imitating the way you walked."

I realized then that our roles had reversed. Now, he had be-come my protector. I realized how angry Jim must have been not just at the kid, but at the accident itself, and I realized, too, how much without ever saying it he loved me and I loved him.

I told my mother what had happened. She had survived my accident fourteen years earlier and my father's death seven years after that. She had raised my brother Tom; overseen her own financial affairs; become a world traveler taking the most demanding trips she could find—riding the Trans-Siberian Railroad, climbing to sixteen thousand feet in the Himalayas; joined and presided over the boards of social service agencies and theater companies. "I never stopped to think about how everyone else was affected," I said.

She looked at me with tears in her eyes and said, "Your accident changed all of us forever."

No one in our family had ever made such a confession or betrayed such a feeling through their actions. Because we had all gone on with our lives, I had never considered that the accident had affected their psyches as permanently as it has affected my body. I had always thought my mother watched me move with a sense of pride and pleasure. After her confession, I looked again. There was indeed pride and pleasure, but there was sadness, too.

My father's first law partner, Judge Nathan Cohen, officiated at the wedding. Jim and Tom were my best men. My friends Bill and Larry and Rens were ushers. So was Dick Woit.

With Kate at my side, I watched Sharon come down the aisle on her brother's arm. She smiled at me the same way she had smiled at Kate that very first night I'd seen her. And for the first time in my life, I believed in miracles.

EPILOGUE

This is how my day begins:

When I am ready to get out of the queen-sized bed I share with Sharon, I take hold of the forest green comforter that keeps my feet warm, but under house arrest. Getting the comforter down far enough to free my legs is difficult. I fly-cast it back and forth until my toes surface. I then bend my left leg toward my chest and arch my back to create a mild spasm that will fool my weaker right leg into imitating its mate. Knees now up, I swivel my hips to the edge of the bed like a break dancer who's lost the rhythm. If I'm lucky, my left leg will lead and the right will have no choice but to follow.

My feet are on the ground now. I bend over and touch the hardwood floor a few times to loosen up. Left palm first, then the right fist, which hasn't bloomed in more than thirty springs.

Loose, but not too loose. After all these years, I can tune my body as if it were a Steinway, albeit a Steinway on which several keys still don't work.

Sitting up straight, I place each hand about six inches from its corresponding thigh, then push hard. One-quarter of the way up, then halfway, then suspended in time and space until I pump my right arm in the air like an oil derrick. Up far enough now to grab the handlebar of the old exercise bike positioned by the bed. I ride the bike at night to keep fit, but use it in the mornings as the first piton to help me inch horizontally across a surface as dangerous to me as the vertical face of a mountain is to a climber. Right hand off bike, left hand on bike, right hand on table, left hand boldly across the three-foot chasm of floor to the bureau. Steady there. Right hand to bathroom door knob. Left hand to the doorframe. Feet up the slight wooden incline onto tile.

Pee, then use the momentum from grabbing the towel bar to get to the sink and then up over the two-inch lip into the shower. We have a walk-in shower, thanks to remodeling about five years ago. You didn't want to see how I got into the bathtub to take a shower the first eight years we lived in this house in Evanston. No matter what time of year, I would slip the fingers of my left hand into the elliptical brass window latch by the end of the tub opposite the showerhead. Unhooking the latch like a clumsy teen unhooking his girlfriend's bra, I'd open the window. My right hand balanced on the high sink behind me, I would then arch my back and swing my left leg over the edge of the tub as if I were mounting a horse. Left hand to the recessed soap holder/saddle horn, right foot up and over—and I'd be in! The window was too far away to close securely. In winter, there would always be a thin layer of ice on the mirror over the sink before I'd finish, shivering always.

Play the videotape in reverse, and I return from shower to bed, where I dress like an old person—seated. Shirt first—a pullover because buttoning is difficult and time-consuming.

Underwear next. Instructions: Pick up the right leg under the knee and place it over the left knee. Pull Jockey's right leg opening up no higher than ankle. Swing right leg back to floor. Insert left leg in opening. Pull both sides of shorts up to thigh. Repeat procedure with blue jeans. Stand, pulling shorts, then jeans into proper position. Sit back down to fasten pants.

Actors in science-fiction movies often must spend several hours each morning in wardrobe and make-up before they are ready to face the cameras. My daily ablutions don't take quite that long. Still, after getting on shirt and pants, I have a long way to go until I can negotiate the day. Before I can put on my shoes and socks and right leg brace, I must stretch my heel cords for about twenty minutes. If I don't, my left leg will buckle under the burden of too much body weight as the tight right leg drags along floor or sidewalk to catch up.

I am not a superstitious man, but stretching the heel cords has become a ritual. I lean on the short but heavy wooden nightstand next to the bed. Hands on the top of the stand, left foot flat on the floor, I get up on the toes of my right foot and put my weight on the foot by rocking back and forth. I count to three hundred, pause, then repeat the exercise for five more sets. If I miscount, I must start over. Right heel done, I switch to the left for six similar sets. Finally, I return to the right. But before starting, I pick up a polished stone from the nightstand that my daughter Nora has given me for good luck. Stone in right hand, I wish luck for those close to me while I complete the stretching. The order and wording is always the same; the beneficiary's name finishes the count to ten. "One-two-three-four-five-six-seven-eight-nine-Rob" (the youngest of my three children, named for my father). Then One-two-three, etc.-

Nora. Then Kate. Then Sharon, my wife. Then me. My brothers and their families. My mother. A friend's wife ill with cancer. Brother-in-law and family. Mother-in-law. And finally, "all my friends and especially ———" (depending on the daily circumstances). If I screw the list up, I start over. If I've done my stretching right and the stone works its magic, we'll all have good, safe days.

Now I can put on my socks. Dressing the right foot is easier because I can swing it over the left knee and roll the sock on with my left hand. I must use my left hand to put on the left sock, too, so that foot remains on the floor while I attempt to lasso it.

Look closely and you'll see that I'm often wearing two different socks—a thin, Argyle one on the left and a thick white one on the right. Socks are my Scylla and Charybdis. Too thick and they inhibit blood flow. Too thin and they inhibit my gait, because the looser my shoe is, the slower the foot pulls through. As I have more difficulty pulling the right leg through, I opt for gait over circulation most mornings. If I need to look "put together"—that is, with matching socks—I will wear a thin sock on the left foot and a matching sock over a second thin sock on the right.

In the 1980s, I did a good deal of sports writing for the *New York Times* and other publications and wrote a book on baseball. Before a game, Detroit Tigers manager Sparky Anderson showed me a yellow legal pad on which he had planned his starting pitching rotation for the next several weeks. He generally used his four starters in the same order, but made important adjustments when possible to account for whom his team might be facing. If, for example, the Tigers were to meet a team with several powerful right-handed hitters, Anderson might strive to keep his left-handed starter on the bench.

I don't have a legal pad, but I rotate my shoes with every bit as much forethought as the baseball manager. I go with a two-shoe rotation. My ace is a sturdy pair of cordovan wing tips. Surgery in which the hard-to-tie laces were removed and replaced with a buckle make the cordovans even more effective. I wear these shoes for three days in a row, after which they become too loose upon my feet (despite the thick socks). My second starter is a heavy black shoe that looks more appropriate for an old man or a teen interning for Doc Martens. These shoes are not as effective as the other pair, but after three straight days of work, the cordovans require two days rest to return to their cozy fit.

When I say "not as effective," I mean that I don't walk as well in them. Everyone's gait and balance alters when they change shoes. Runners certainly notice the difference, as do women switching from heels to flats. I'm put together by chewing gum, rubber bands, and Elmer's glue, anyway; doctors and therapists find it hard to believe that I can walk at all given my strength, or lack thereof. I use a cane and rely heavily on balance. But if that balance is thrown off by, say, a change in the height of the heel or the angle of the sole, I can easily fall.

I still wear a brace on my right leg, although now it is plastic. The L-shaped orthotic, molded to fit the contour of my calf and foot, slips into the shoe and runs from toes to just below the knee. It is designed to keep my foot from "dropping." Still, every couple of months, I must visit Mike the shoemaker for new leather soles to replace those worn down by my foot-dragging. (Rubber soles are out of the question; they catch on the floor too easily.) If Mike takes more than a few days, I'm sometimes forced to rely on a third pair—my relief shoes. Actually, they are low boots that are angled so differently from heel to toe than my other shoes that it takes a couple of hours before I feel comfortable and safe walking in them.

When I know I must be at an event that requires a lot of walking or just time on my feet, I make adjustments to my rotation just as manager Anderson did. I know I will want my cordovans "on the mound"—fresh, not working for the second or third day in a row and too loose to support me. So, a week in advance of the event, I'll adjust my lineup to assure that the cordovans will be at their best.

By the time I walk the fifteen or so feet from bedroom door to stairway, I can tell whether my heel cords are still too tight. My left leg will send the SOS that it might go AWOL due to the additional pressure it is bearing. If the cords are still tight and I have time, I return for more stretching before taking the sixteen stairs from second floor to first. If I'm in a hurry, I make a mental note to monitor the left leg's strength just as I monitor the surface on which I am walking and scores of other variables. I recently saw a car commercial in which the viewer is taken into the mind of the driver as he gleefully speeds down a challenging road. At the same time, the viewer is taken into the "mind" of the car. A series of scientific equations pop up on the screen as the car handles curves and avoids obstacles. I'm like the car when I'm walking. Factoring in data. All business. No emotion.

Today I am comfortable in my cordovans. My heel cords are well stretched. I've fingered the stone for luck for family, friends, and self. Still, whenever I'm walking, I look like I might crash at any moment. As a result, the road I travel is paved with people with good intentions.

Sharon and I were recently in a museum when a young woman in an official maroon museum blazer approached. She turned to Sharon and asked: "Would he like a wheelchair?"

This was not the first time that someone had asked my wife this kind of question in my presence. Over the years I have heard restaurant hostesses ask her if I would prefer a booth or table; movie ushers ask her if I would like to enter the theater early; people on stairways ask her if I would like any help climbing. Indeed, a few weeks before our trip to the museum, a similarly blazered passenger representative had also asked, "Would he like a wheelchair?" as we came off an airplane at O'Hare.

To tell the truth, there are plenty of times when I would like a wheelchair: when my son's Little League game is on a field that is too far away from the parking lot and I end up sitting in the car watching his barely identifiable figure from a vantage point as unsatisfactory as the Goodyear Blimp's; and, yes, when we touch down at an O'Hare gate so far away from the terminal that it has a different zip code. On these occasions and many others, I think to myself how easy it would be to be pushed once in a while instead of always feeling the need to push myself. But I don't allow it. To me, riding in a wheelchair, even if only briefly, remains the first step to slipping backward.

Sharon knew the only answer to give the airline representative: "No thanks. He won't ride in a wheelchair."

I was not angered by the substance of this stranger's offer, but I was annoyed by the way in which the offer had been made. "I'm tired of people speaking to me through you," I said to Sharon. "Next time tell them to ask me directly."

"Why don't you tell them?" she replied.

I confess that in the days that followed, I had been waiting for the opportunity to do just that. Now, this well-meaning soul from the museum had provided the opening. I pivoted, then put my free arm in front of Sharon as I might put it in front of one of my children as we approached a dangerous intersection. "Why don't you ask me?" I said loudly. The words echoed through the hall, focusing attention on us that under ordinary circumstances would have disturbed me. Because I am a moving gaper's block, I generally try to remain as invisible as possible in public.

The young woman started to respond, but I cut her off. "Why would you talk to me through my wife? Do you think that because I'm on a cane I can't talk? I went to college. I went to law school. I practiced law. I've written books. I *have* a voice."

I have spent the last thirty-plus years trying to lead a normal life, trying to show by my actions that I may be different but I am whole. With the passage of time, marriage, and children, I have learned the corny truth that society can only work if we understand one another. You can't know me or the millions of other Americans who walk differently than you, talk differently than you, or look different than you unless you hear our voices. You can't know if we share the same dreams and fears as you unless you hear our stories. You can't know what we want or how we feel unless you ask. Us.

Are my dreams the same as yours? As I write this, I am forty-eight years old, the same age my father was when he died almost twenty-five years ago. The youngest of my three children is the same age that my brother Tom was when my father died. I dream first and foremost of watching all of my children grow to adulthood and sharing the joy of that with my wife— an opportunity my father never had.

And yet I know from experience that there are no promises.

Your life can change forever in the blink of an eye that it takes to hit a wrestling mat the wrong way. You can drop dead before you are fifty. Two winters ago, as I walked across a street, I was hit by a car that ran a red light. The car was going thirty miles an hour. I saw it coming. There was nothing I could do. My life did not pass before my eyes, but I was certain I was going to die.

I didn't. My right leg—the weak one—was badly shattered. My right arm—the weak one—was broken at the elbow. Surgery was necessary. By chance, I knew the orthopedic surgeon at the hospital to which I was brought. He was David Beigler, a fellow Woit's Warrior. Before I fell asleep from the anesthetic, I allowed myself to cry for the first and only time. "You know what I'm willing to do to get better," I said to David. "Just put me back together. I'll do the rest."

The stakes were just as high this time as they had been in 1967. Maybe higher. I had not only my life ahead of me; I had the lives of my wife and children to worry about. The doctor did his job, and I did mine. I'm just as good (or bad) as I was before the car hit me.

This summer will mark the fortieth anniversary of my trip to Yankee Stadium. My kids have inherited my love of the game. Kate, who was six when her mom and I wed, spent her formative years in box seats behind the White Sox dugout at the old Comiskey Park. Nora, who was born in 1984—the year after the Sox earned their first postseason berth since 1959—has the distinction of recording the first strikeout in the history of the newly formed girls' fast-pitch league in our community. Rob, who followed in 1987, plays catcher, third base, and outfield for the Skokie Indians, a local traveling all-star team.

Not too long ago, with a family driving trip to the Baseball

Hall of Fame postponed due to Little League playoffs, we took a short vacation at a modest resort in Galena, Illinois. When Rob learned that Galena was only an hour from the "if you build it, he will come" Field of Dreams, he asked if we could make the trip.

We drove across the Iowa border in tandem with another family, close friends whose two boys love baseball as much as our kids do. Dubuque. Bankston. Cornfields. Dyersville. More cornfields. Just like in the movie, the field appears out of nowhere.

By chance this was Fantasy Camp week at the field. Many of the dozen or so ex–major-leaguers on hand dated back to my own childhood. Mudcat Grant. Bert Campaneris. Jimmy "The Toy Cannon" Wynn. And Ryne Duren, the fast, but wild, reliever who had pitched for my beloved Yankees for four seasons, including the year I visited the ballpark. Nora, Rob, and their friends Nat and Elie had heard of only a handful of these men, now in their fifties and sixties; but a ballplayer is a ballplayer. The kids rushed off for autographs as if Ryne Duren were Ryne Sandberg.

After the fantasy campers had broken for lunch, the diamond opened to the general public. Gloves on, our children joined a half-dozen others and a few adults in the field. A man in his thirties stood at home plate and hit pop flies to the assembled.

I stood with Sharon on the sidelines, my strong left hand on my cane, my weak right hand in hers. The batter lofted the ball high into the air. Rob camped under it and waited. The ball seemed to float up into the cloudless blue sky forever. Long enough for me to think that life will never be any better than this.

ACKNOWLEDGMENTS

Three Quarters, Two Dimes, and a Nickel would not have been possible if several people hadn't contributed their two cents. I am in debt to Ira Berkow, who years ago encouraged me to follow my dreams (and who had the foresight to see that I'd eventually write a book on this subject). I owe just as much to my literary agent, Gail Hochman, for her generosity of spirit, her support, and her persistence, not to mention her excellent editorial guidance. The contributions of my editor, now friend, Paul Golob, can hardly be quantified. Paul not only pushed me to write the book; he pushed me to write it honestly. Remarkably, he knew where it was going before I did—and he made sure it got there. My three children, Kate, Nora, and Robert, were, as always, supportive, understanding, and inspirational. A special thanks to the remarkable Dick Woit. Finally, I owe my greatest thanks to my wife, Sharon, for all she has contributed—not just to this book (which was considerable), but to my life.

About the Author

STEVE FIFFER was born in Chicago in 1950 and is a graduate of Yale University and of the University of Chicago School of Law. He is the author of seven previous books, including the award-winning *A Season for Justice*, written with Morris Dees, and *So You've Got a Great Idea*. He is also the coeditor, with his wife Sharon Sloan Fiffer, of the acclaimed collections *Home: American Writers Remember Rooms of Their Own* and *Family: American Writers Remember Their Own*. A frequent contributor to the *New York Times* and to *Chicago Magazine*, he lives with his wife and three children in Evanston, Illinois.